RUGGERO D'ALESSANDRO AND LUCA SALTINI

THE LAND OF SPACE AND DUST

A Trip to the U.S.A. with 13 Writers 1920-2000

MIMESIS
INTERNATIONAL

© 2024 – MIMESIS INTERNATIONAL
www.mimesisinternational.com
e-mail: info@mimesisinternational.com

Isbn: 9788869774638
Book series: *Literature* n. 15

© MIM Edizioni Srl
P.I. C.F. 02419370305

CONTENTS

A NOVEL IDEA

In *Hamlet*, Shakespeare has the protagonist's most faithful friend say that 'words capable of making stones sensitive' are needed. It is a very evocative image that can be applied to the whole of art - a term that includes literature and poetry, painting and music, film, and sculpture.

During a life dedicated to work and family, fatigue and commitment, the space dedicated by 'ordinary' people to so-called 'culture' is generally understood as pure entertainment, comprising a few (rarely all) of these genres: cassette films, low-quality TV, a few books chosen based on sales charts and showcase that attract customers (rather than readers), big-name exhibitions and concerts.

If we think of a person who wants to take up reading (regardless of age and social class, occupation, and qualification), the question arises as to how and why he or she gets into romance novels or 19th century English literature, detective or spy stories, adventure stories or Joyce's complete works. Why would he/she choose the best-selling (in 2013/14) *Fifty Shades* or throw himself headlong into Proust, rather than into Ian Fleming (by the way, the complete work is currently being published in Italy by Adelphi, a classic attribution of a quarter of nobility to an author who until now has been underestimated as merely 'the father of 007')? We do not intend to deal with issues that concern sociology of culture and market statistics, the marketing strategies of the major publishing houses. The point is that when we talk about the novel in the 1910s, we must bear in mind that we are talking about a genre within an act, that of reading, and within a society with profoundly different characteristics from those marking, for example, the 1920s or 1950s, not to mention even earlier eras.

To put it simply, we are interested in putting ourselves on the writer's side, rather than the reader's one, and reflecting on the relationship between writing stories and doing so while living in a specific historical period, society, and culture. Let us read what the journalist Giovanna Zucconi and the novelist Jonathan Franzen, speaking of 'high art', the opposite, that is, of the 'culture as entertainment' mentioned at the beginning:

> his novel was and is 'high art', not TV stuff. But elitism is the worst sin in America: hence the broadside of insults (...) "What can I do?" he says. 'People buy it. They like it. Yet I didn't write it for the general public. I made no compromises. (...) To write it, he locked himself for years in a small flat in New York, in the dark, 'because you can find the keys on the computer anyway', and to really write, to tell the story of an era and a country, you don't need to see the world but only to sharpen your sensitivity.[1]

Is what the author of *The Corrections* says about narrating a country and an era true? What seems interesting to us is not the fact of locking oneself up in the house or living on the street to be able to write, but rather the concept of 'high art' (as it happens, it is the same author of the journalistic piece who isolates this concept, so much discussed by decades of sociology of culture and mass media studies, with inverted commas). It is significant that a highly successful writer like Franzen talks about rejecting compromises and writing with the general public in mind. Equally significant is the particular character of this author, who is certainly situated in the sphere of 'high' literature, but at the same time a very fashionable and widely read phenomenon for almost fifteen years.

While writing his third novel (*The Corrections*, 2001), he is crossed by two thoughts that are as essential as they are recurrent: on the one hand he recounts one of the main subjects of all universal literature - the family - and not from the sociological or psychological, political or group psychoanalysis profile, but of those who are or have been part of it (hence anyone who reads the book); on the other hand, he faces the problem, now dramatic for him, of trying to 'break

---

1   G. Zucconi, *Lo strambo dell'America*, La Stampa, 17 April 2002.

through', considering the very little success met by his first two novels (*The Twenty-Seventh City*, 1988 and *Strong Motion*, 1992).

In the United States of the 1990s (even more so today, 20 years later), writing in the hope of being published, reviewed, read, and appreciated by critics and the public is an extremely complicated operation, halfway between luck and talent, imagination and nerve, self-confidence and winning literary marketing strategies, and the desire to show off but with as few compromises as possible (if there are some values to preserve).

We hear Franzen again talk about topics such as 'entertaining in the least detrimental sense' and the desire readers may or may not have to spend time with a writer, that is, with his work:

> It is true that *The Corrections* bears no traces of the formal experimentalisms and metanarrative reflections typical of Modernism.

My main aim is to entertain the audience in the least detrimental sense of the word. In the twentieth century, writers took it for granted that the novel was something important and could therefore write about the novel within the novel itself. But writers of my generation cannot so confidently assume that readers want to spend time with them. Today the novel and culture are marginal phenomena ... there are other diversions. When Henry James wrote *The Ambassadors* or *The Golden Bowl* he was sure to find readers who would follow him. Today it is different: in a certain sense we have to win back an audience. Don't sound like a blind calculation ... believe me, I am also speaking as a reader.[2]

Whatever one thinks of what the author of *The Corrections* explained, there is no doubt that the novel genre has lagged behind, and not a little, in terms of social and cultural relevance compared to the days of Dickens or those of Hemingway.

We will deal in this short book with writers who talk about society and at the same time live in society - and not necessarily the former coinciding with the latter. What effects are produced by this absolutely unavoidable link for anyone? Everyone comes from a family, lives

---

2   *J. Franzen, L'America di J. Franzen.* Intervista di Susanna Battisti, http://www. kwlibri.kataweb.it/meeting/meeting_230402.shtml.

in a given society; and if writers represent a very small proportion of the population of each country, it is nevertheless true that all writers are also readers. Dealing with the writer-society relationship does not mean looking for social echoes in writing, let alone tracing the political coordinates of the writer or conjuring up improbable revolutionary or conservative agendas between the lines of novels and short stories. On the contrary, if one deals with novelists who are worth dealing with - insofar as they are capable of 'writing words that make stones sensitive', as we said at the beginning - there will be nothing programmatic, searching or unashamedly ideological in those words. If there is one thing the literary (and other) avant-gardes of the 20th century teach, it is precisely to steer clear of programmes and ideologies: only by sincerely recounting what has never been recounted or in the way it has never been recounted does one make literature. This too, after all, is politics, in the sense of a discourse on individual and common living (*pòlis, communitas*).

Even starting with a simple piece of earth from which to one day cover what will remain of oneself, one can arrive at the most intense and vivid literature:

> It all started when I was looking for a place for my grave, says Philip Roth about Sabbath Theatre, his most desperate, free, and mocking book.[3]

The choice of the United States and its literature, limited (so to speak) to just under a century - from 1920 to the present - is anything but random; and for a good number of good reasons.

The States were once called 'America' to simplify and at the same time highlight, in amazement, the completely 'other' dimension with respect to our country: just think of the role played in the imagination and cultural formation of groups of young people educated by a book like Americana, edited in 1941 for Bompiani by Elio Vittorini. It may therefore be interesting to unearth a few scattered traces of this distant yet revived myth with each new film or musical, IT or commercial release.

---

3   M.R. Bricchi, *Philip Roth. Biografia nonostante l'autore*, Il Sole 24 ore, 15 December 2013.

Secondly, the geographic density of a country/continent like the United States (already declared programmatically by its very name) can be weighed and appreciated by the provenance of its writers, the landscapes they evoke, the characters they relate, the local accents they echo. Steinbeck is inseparable from California, as much as Faulkner and O'Connor represent two of the greatest voices of the Deep South, while Salinger's New York is quite different from the one recounted by Roth or Auster. How much society our dozen authors tell, while at the same time speaking always and differently about the United States.[4]

Moreover, moving from the discovery of talent and the cultivation of style to topics such as the literature and market relations, questioning the changing role of the writer with the changing times, or the cruel reality of no less than four wars (the two world wars, Korea and Vietnam), adding the expeditions to Iraq and Afghanistan, the presence of troops and military 'advisers' in numerous countries in Central and South America, all constitute an exercise in culture as a lived life, which is as fruitful and complex as ever in a world such as the US.

As for the choice of thirteen writers, it is certainly no more justifiable than other choices; especially considering the extreme wealth of US literary talent over the past 90 years. Instead, it is a choice dictated by what is perhaps the best motivation: personal taste. As for those who will complain about the absence of names such as John Dos Passos or Woody Guthrie, we can quietly reply that we are not interested in dealing with authors who are directly

---

4   For very useful historical support, consider M.A. Jones, *Storia degli Stati Uniti d'America. Dalle prime colonie inglesi ai giorni nostri*, Bompiani, Milano 1995. For a fascinating spatial and geographical perspective that cannot be renounced (like all his works): F. Moretti, *La letteratura vista da lontano*, Einaudi, Torino 2005. On the subject of stratification and social conflicts, he writes: 'the class struggle in the countryside, the industrial take-off, and the process of state centralisation have transformed (and unravelled) the form of the 19th-century idyll. In the great laboratory of history, of which the maps in their way provide us with a logbook, the 'external' force of these great socio-political processes is the independent variable that acts on the narrative structure and reveals the direct relationship - tangible, at times - between social conflict and aesthetic form'.
Cf. Moretti, *La letteratura...*, cit., p. 82.

involved in politics while they write (let it be said without any controversy). Moreover, our thirteen include the author of one of the most intense social portraits of the 20th century, the Steinbeck of *The Grapes of Wrath* (1939).[5]

Even the styles of approaching the authors themselves are different, determined only by our personal quest for understanding. In fact, each of us followed his own path and approached a writer first since our need to understand. The articles reflect this personal quest and do not follow a uniform pattern. What binds each page is the love of literature and the undiminished faith in the power of the novel. In this regard, on the value of the novel form, one of the best reflections seems to us to be that of the Peruvian Nobel Prize winner Vargas Llosa, an example of a writer of conservative ideas and at the same time of rare intensity and poetry:

> Nothing defends the living being against the stupidity of prejudice, racialism, xenophobia, localist obtuseness, religious or political sectarianism, or discriminatory nationalism better than the unbroken constant that always appears in great literature: the essential equality of men and women in all latitudes and the injustice represented by establishing forms of discrimination, dependency, or exploitation between them. Nothing, better than good novels, teaches us to see in ethnic and cultural differences the richness of human heritage and to appreciate them as a manifestation of its many creativity.[6]

Note

The idea for this book came from both authors, nourished by exchanges of ideas, corrections, doubts and above all enthusiasm. The historical introduction in chapters 1 and 2 and the paragraphs

---

5   *Regarding political engagement*, see: A. Donno, *Dal New Deal alla guerra fredda. Aspetti del radicalismo statunitense negli anni '40*, Sansoni, Florence 1983.

6   M. Vargas Llosa, *È possibile pensare il mondo moderno senza il romanzo?*, in F. Moretti (ed.), *Il romanzo. Volume I: La cultura del romanzo*, Einaudi, Turin 2001, p. 5.

on Hemingway, Faulkner, Steinbeck, Fante, O'Connor and Kerouac were written by Luca Saltini.

The paragraphs on Fitzgerald, Salinger and Carver, as well as the entire third chapter, are the work of Ruggero D'Alessandro.

PART I
WHERE AUTHORS AND CHARACTERS LIVE
Fitzgerald, Hemingway, Faulkner, Steinbeck, Fante

1
THE UNITED STATES
BETWEEN THE TWO WORLD WARS

What did the Great War mean for the people who were involved in it? What was the impact on the imagination and conscience of people living in Europe at the time? The tragic images of the conflict deeply entered people's souls. Millions died in the absurd battles of the trenches, thousands were maimed, traumatised, those who were wiped out by the Spanish, in addition to the serious destruction suffered by the various states, with countries razed to the ground, factories wiped out, infrastructure compromised. The cost in both economic terms and of human lives was very high for a Europe waking up from the nightmare in a world that had become unfamiliar, where the old balances were shocked forever.

The United States was left out of this drama, or almost. It was not until 1917, with a limited number of men, that the conflict offered the huge American production machine the opportunity to exploit its full potential, now revolutionised by the new industrial concept inspired by Taylorism. US territory had been spared by the war. The soldiers returned home and found nothing to rebuild, nor did they face unemployment and economic crisis. Instead, they discovered endless possibilities for a new future, all to be invented. The country found itself thrown into the roarin' twenties, years when the American dream seemed to be realised at its best.

Industrial production rose by 64% in a few years, the large warehouses grew from 29,000 to 160,000, the dividends of the major companies increased by 65% in the short space of time between 1923 and 1929. The standard of living of the population rose to the rhythm of the Charleston and the new jazz music, running on the tyres of Model T Fords and over the airwaves of radios, which were now widespread. These were also the years of big Wall Street business where making money seemed so easy, the age of skyscrapers and the age of Rudolph Valentino's Hollywood. Beneath this shiny image, however, American society concealed deep tensions.

The participation in the world war was not seen by the general public as an opportunity for the country, but was read by many in connection with the civil war. The still fresh experience had left a broad aftermath in the population, a sense of physical and psychological trauma that made intervention in the European war seem merely a useless sacrifice. The horrors of the Marne, of Verdun, of Caporetto, revived dormant fears and joined the wound of an event like the Argonne counter-offensive, where the United States recorded over 100,000 casualties. The men in the street had the feeling that they were fighting to defend the interests of a big business, not of ordinary people. The world that emerged from the conflict looked shattered and impossible to recompose. Important authors such as Dos Passos, Cummings, Hemingway, or Faulkner interpreted this disillusionment and anguish.

On a more strictly economic level, the wages and living standards of Americans did indeed rise during the 1920s, but at the cost of increasing exploitation of workers and greater job insecurity. Moreover, the purchasing power of the population did not increase at the same rate as production. In 1929, of the 27.5 million American households, 21.5 had an income of less than USD 3,000 a year and, of these, 6 million did not even reach USD 1,000. Against this backdrop, there was a noticeable increase in the migration of black people from the South of the country to the big cities in the North. The newcomers were concentrated in huge urban ghettos, such as Harlem in New York or the South Side in Chicago. By the end of the decade, about 40% of black Americans lived in these deprived neighbourhoods.

All this was fuelling strong social pressure, which was combined with the fear of red scare, unleashed after the waves of strikes in 1919 and resulted in serious repressive measures against individual freedom: searches, detentions, arrests, forced repatriation of foreigners, summary trials, such as that of Sacco and Vanzetti. All this favoured the revival of a climate of racism and fear of the 'enemy within', which coagulated around phenomena such as the Ku Klux Klan.

This created a sharp split in the heart of American society between the world of business, finance, and politics, which recognised the international involvement of the United States as an irreversible fact of life, and a real society that was increasingly worried by these openings and inclined to withdraw into itself. All these contradictions exploded most violently in 1929.

The collapse of the Wall Street stock market and the onset of the most serious economic crisis the country had ever experienced swept away all the golden patina in a few moments of the 1920s and revealed the ills of a system that was thought to be prosperous. Thousands of banks closed their doors, over 74 billion dollars were burnt, 85,000 companies went bankrupt, the unemployed rose from 3.5 million in 1930 to 16 million three years later. Ford, for example, reduced its workforce from 128,000 to 37,000 in two years. More than 300,000 families were left homeless, 750,000 farms were abandoned, violence, delinquency, and vagrancy grew, young people were left in their own hands, families started to travel from one part of the country to another, in a context symbolically marked by long and desperate queues for bread.

Unemployment not only affected the working classes and peasants, but also swept over the middle classes, who had believed themselves to have reached a state of security. Their wages were slashed and their jobs mowed down. Feelings of dismay and loneliness, anger at broken promises and the failure of national values, as well as fear of an uncertain future, matured in the populace. It was in this undergrowth that the complex and contradictory culture of the 1930s developed, which turned out to be particularly vital and was able to contribute not only to the country's recovery, but also to its renaissance in a more social and democratic sense.

The measures launched by Roosevelt from 1933 onwards as part of the New Deal succeeded in partly absorbing the great unemployment, especially with the huge public works programme of which those in the Tennessee valley are the most resounding. Alongside this, however, there was a revival in the people's desire to know and investigate things, fostering the rise of a mass cultural industry.

In the 1930s, American cinema reached its zenith, not only providing brief escapes for a population full of worries, but also imposing new models of the citizen - honest, hard-working, opposed to the gangsters who moved about in many cities with a recklessness never to be seen again. Many films denounced the most unbridled capitalism, the dehumanisation of Taylorism (think of Chaplin's classic works *City Lights* and *Modern Times*), the excesses and imbalances of that society.

In literature, impressive paradigm shifts took place, such as Steinbeck's novels, culminating in the celebrated *The Grapes of Wrath*, but also John O'Hara's short stories, Faulkner's *The Sound and the Fury*, or Howard Fast's works, such as *Citizen Tom Paine* and *The Last Frontier*, which questioned the myth of the conquest of the West, anticipating in many ways the Liberal culture of the 1960s and 1970s.

The decade of the 1930s is also the decade of the revival of jazz, healing the wounds of a beaten down and defeated America. It is the time of the limelight of the greats of this scene, Duke Ellington, Benny Goodman, Billie Holiday, to name a few. Jazz orchestras flourished, as well as orchestras of other African-American genres, helping to increase the participation of this part of the population in the cultural life of the country. The blacks themselves were able to develop a new consciousness of their civil rights, which, however, did not find fruitful development until the 1960s.

2
"WHATEVER I WRITE CANNOT BE UGLY".
FRANCIS SCOTT FITZGERALD

2.1 *Fitzgerald between stylistic research and social analysis*

A theme such as style becomes a problem in every writer, to the point of being able to say: the better he is, the more the problem of 'making style' arises. The choice of the verb 'make' is intended to refer to the idea and the concrete space of the workshop where each book is made. And do not think of a subject far removed from the spaces of the society in which the animator of this workshop lives. The sentence quoted as the title of this paragraph would be a declaration of complete arrogance on the lips of any person: but not of a writer recognised as such, first and foremost by himself - in this case Francis Scott Fitzgerald.

It is also to him that Pavese thinks when he speaks of the United States - or rather of America as it was known in the 1930s and 1940s - as a utopian land, yet deeply anchored in the analysis of the real land. Jay Gatsby's luxurious mansion set in a landscape reminiscent of the equally luxurious Hamptons is one of the most ambiguous portions of such a land, as utopian as it is real. A utopia like Jay's desperate, volatile love for Daisy, set beside the real gunshot that kills him drifting in his immense pool:

> America. Periods of discontent have often seen the emergence of the literary myth of a country proposed as a term of comparison, a Germany recreated by a Tacitus or a Stael. Often, the uncovered country is only a land of utopia, a social allegory that hardly has anything in common with the existing country; it is no less useful for that.[1]

---

1   C. Pavese, *La letteratura americana e altri saggi*, Einaudi, Turin 1951, p. XIII

The consciousness of writing, the self-consciousness of knowing how to do it very well, is also the social springboard of becoming a writer. Becoming anything that happens in life: fame, success, decadence, alcoholism, 'hole hands', ruin, self-destruction, premature death.

A painful path in which natural talent (like Mozart for composing, Einstein for physics, Gould for the piano) lives its own life of disbelief, acclaim, waste, compromises with the market, success, final misunderstanding, and *post-mortem* canonisation. It is a path that Sergio Perosa analyses well in the long introduction to the important Italian edition of Fitzgerald's *Notebooks*:

> Friends and acquaintances could not understand. They looked at Fitzgerald with disbelief, distrust, sometimes with ill-concealed irritation. He had not completed his studies, and would always have had some uncertainty about spelling; he led a frivolous life, his affairs with Zelda fed the worldly news and tabloid magazines, and he wrote openly to make money and aim for popular success. For Edmund Wilson, his university companion, later to become his 'intellectual conscience', he represented a phenomenon of custom; but he also represented the mystery of artistic excellence that lurks among the dustiest refuse. For Hemingway (...) he was the example of a natural talent, of the genuine writer with a sure and happy nose.[2]

The 'charmer with words', to quote the author of *The 49 Stories* again, takes on the most disparate guises: the young journalist, adventurer, fishing and boxing enthusiast, collector of women (Hemingway); the restless landowner, seduced in his youth by the Paris of the *Lost Generation* together with the two aforementioned colleagues, perplexed at receiving the Nobel Prize announcement

---

2   S. Perosa, *Introduzione*, in F.S. Fitzgerald, *I taccuini*, Einaudi, Turin 1980, p. V. On the relationship between the writer and American society in the 1920s and 1930s, here is what two Anglo-Americanists wrote: 'Fitzgerald was never really accepted by the social world he describes in his novels, and he remained an outsider all his life, also because he was aware of the spiritual emptiness, the desperation and the sterility of this pleasure-seeking, irresponsible society. M. Raimondi Capasso and R. Fiotta Genova, *Cross-Sections. A Socio-Literary Survey of British and American Cultural Traditions*, Ghisetti e Corvi Editori, Milan 1981, p. 685.

while working on his property like any other direct farmer (Faulkner); the unsuccessful doctor, able to tell the story of the anti-Nazi resistance in Norway like the endless arable land of Salinas (Steinbeck); or the extravagant post-modernist experimenter, who has been missing from the news since the late 1950s and appears in a comic strip with a sack over his head in an episode of *The Simpsons'* while his face is unknown (Pynchon).

But for the 20-year-old Scott, knowing how to write is equivalent to two or three fundamental things for his future life: fame, winning over his beloved Zelda Sayre - the belle of the village, balancing the failure to graduate from Princeton, making him forget his lack of talent for sports, as well as his failure to leave for the European front in the First World War. As we can see, these aspects can be read as a coin: the deep, personal, self-conquering side; the social side, being considered, admired, envied, show/show-off, up to the consumerist follies of what the Norwegian-born sociologist Thorstein Veblen calls 'conspicuous consumption' - the luxurious villa in New England, the property on the French Riviera, the luxury hotels in New York, Paris, Rome and London, the drinking, *The Diamond as Big as the Ritz*.[3]

It is interesting to quote one of the best analysts and critics of state society in the first half of the 20th century who, not surprisingly, refers to Veblen:

---

3   See Veblen's sociological masterpiece, *La teoria della classe agiata*, Einaudi, Turin 1971. For a profile of the social scientist we refer to R. D'Alessandro, *La società vistosa. Attualità di Veblen*, Critica marxista, bimonthly, September-October 2011, pp. 41-50 (double column). The short story The Diamond as Big as the Ritz is included in F.S. Fitzgerald's collection, *Racconti dell'età del jazz*, Mondadori, Milan 1980, pp. 191-253. It is very likely that the author of *The Great Gatsby* would have subscribed to what Roth said at the (voluntary) end of his artistic career: 'At the end of his life the boxer Joe Louis said, 'I did the best I could with what I had'. It's exactly what I would say of my work: I did the best I could with what I had'. "After that, I decided that I was finished with fiction (…) I dedicated my life to the novel. I studied them. I taught them. I wrote them, and I read them. At the exclusion of nearly everything else. It's enough! D. Remnick, *Philip Roth Says Enough*, The New Yorker, November 9, 2012.

The American society of Veblen's generation (...) most writers described a disorderly and ruthless economic system, wasteful and inhuman, unfair to workers as well as to capital investors and consumers, politically corrupt and morally corrupting.

This far from unanimous repudiation of the accepted economic order by its literary representatives is one of the curious phenomena of American culture. The tradition of protest and revolt had been dominant in American literature since Emerson and Thoreau.[4]

Fitzgerald was fully aware, even before others (and of Hemingway himself, in some respects more mature than his friend-rival), of the wasteful and disordered background of the *American way of life*, of the randomness of so many successes, and he savoured their ruthlessness (the episode he experienced together with his last companion is exemplary, when he hears young people coming out of a theatre where one of his plays is being performed confess that they thought Fitzgerald was long dead).

Clearly bachelor and chronic alcoholic, frivolously desperate and spendthrift, failed graduate, and social climber: yet capable better than others of social analysis, of his own time, of the much-vaunted Roaring Twenties. In this sense, works such as *The Beautiful and Damned* and *The Great Gatsby* stand worthily alongside the works of Veblen and Lynd, Commager, and Dewey as a commentary on the events and social temperature of America between the two world wars.[5]

And fundamental in this great creative operation is the process of stylistic concern mentioned above, thus profoundly linked to

---

4   H.S. Commager, *Lo spirito americano*, La Nuova Italia, Florence 1951, pp. 273-74.

5   "Democratic prose validates equality and narrates 'the common hero', 'capitalism (which is a different thing from democracy) offers [great individuality] a new and immense field of application'. *The Great Gatsby* tells of precisely this new field offered by capitalism to the poetic principles once associated with the old European aristocracy. For readers, Gatsby represents what Daisy represents for him: the poetic side of capital, the relationship between money and beauty, imagination, romance, creativity'. M.P. Ginsburg and L.G. Nandrea, *La prosa del mondo. 4. America terra della prosa L'americano, Il grande Gatsby*, in F. Moretti (ed.), *Il romanzo. Volume Quarto: Temi, luoghi, eroi*, Einaudi, Turin 2003, p. 105.

the living, active, sensitive antenna of that time and society. Perosa writes again:

> In this (...) he sees deeper or more lucidly than the novelists who flocked up behind him and would shortly afterwards conquer the limelight, with Hemingway in the lead. And he does so with poignant felicity of writing, a magic touch and measure, the deployment of very few means. After the muddled and jumbled models of H.G. Wells and Dreiser followed in the first two novels, he discovered the technical lesson of Henry James (the circumscribed point of view, such as the presenting and 'foreshortening' the story from Nick's point of view) and Conrad's (the deliberate chronological rhyming, the suggestiveness of the musical phrase or symbolic extension).[6]

2.2 *Boats against the current. Time and writing in Fitzgerald*

In the volume that collects the notebooks, the writer gives some examples of conversations and phrases collected here and there; but in reality they are very good demonstrations of the inimitable Fitzgerald style. To three of the many passages in this paragraph we add what is perhaps the most famous sentence written by the author of Gatsby, and which concludes this specific novel:

> The man's life was a kind of dream, as are almost all lives whose mainspring has been left out.
> Suddenly her face summed up that expression that can only come from a careful and repeated study of film magazines and can only be described as a long blonde aspiration for something, the aspiration for a marriage made with Shirley Temple's youth, Clark Gable's earning power, Clark Gable's love and Charles Laughton's talent - and with a bright smile the girl disappeared.
> We cannot allow our worlds to crumble around us like a quantity of dropped trays.[7]

---

6   Perosa, *Introduzione...*, cit., pp. VI-VII.
7   Fitzgerald, *I taccuini...*, cit., p. 21.

So, we proceed with difficulty, boats against the current, relentlessly pushed back into the past.[8]

Life as a dream (an unintentional reference to Calderon's *La vida es sueño*) is one of the characteristics of both Fitzgerald's stories and of the 'Jazz Age' itself, the era that unfolds frenetically and illusorily between the Peace of Versailles and Wall Street's *Black Friday* in October 1929. The 'spring left out' indicates the absence of a strong ethic, a proceeding as a 'bar-which against the current', with time stalking relentlessly, a sort of wind that makes every step forward tiring. And here the first sentence in a programmatic *tout se tient* relates to the closing of the most famous novel (not necessarily the best; our modest predilection goes more to *The Beautiful and Damned*, followed by *The Last Tycoon*).

Turning briefly to the other two passages quoted here too, we can connect them well. Youth and money, talent and love oscillate inconstantly during life, with Fitzgerald unconsciously mixing them up, impersonating them in three actor figures. Thus, if even love and talent are far removed from the passing youth and money, which are ambiguous and often the result of theft or trafficking or cynicism, the reconnection of them with two actors (even if unmistakable with the spoilt and neurotic Temple, in particular the brilliant Laughton) is an operation that tends to rarefy even love and talent, to make them transient and relative. Everything has a flavour of *papier-mâché*, like the huge Hollywood sign placed in the 1920s on the hill above Los Angeles, an illusion of one of the most illusory myths of modernity. And yet it is precisely the United States that created the 'magnificent obsession' (to quote the title of Douglas Sirk's 1954 film, which since the 1960s has become the favourite way for cinephiles to refer to the object of their passion), that made it the first trademark of the 'American century' - even before jazz and Coca-cola, detective novels and comics. And as chance would have it, Fitzgerald's own attempted adventure in Hollywood foundered in extreme failure in the second half of the 1930s. It was the golden age of a film industry

---

8   F.S. Fitzgerald, *Il grande Gatsby*, Newton Compton, Rome 1989, p. 186.

incapable of appreciating the refined talent of the former literary *enfant prodige* of the previous decade.[9]

Rightly so, Fernanda Pivano - author of some of the best pages of Fitzgerald criticism - recalls how the last three years of the writer's life were marked by desperate work in Hollywood, years among the most bitter, the message in a bottle of a survivor of the crash of '29. Even to the very end, he remains conscious of his talent, as is shown by what he says to an acquaintance and mediocre writer:

> You know, I used to be very talented. It was a wonderful feeling to know that I had it, and it hasn't disappeared completely yet. I think I have enough left in me to be able to crank out a couple more novels. I may have to crank them out thin, and they won't be as good as my best stuff. But they won't be completely ugly either, because whatever I write cannot be ugly at all.[10]

The lucid self-analysis of a 44-year-old man a few months before his untimely death, an alcoholic for almost twenty years, with his incurable wife in a psychiatric clinic and a great success behind him for ten years, is both tender and admiring. Three weeks before his death, from his third and fatal heart attack, he writes to his teenage daughter Scottie about working slowly and less but having a great time. Her human drama is of no interest to the public, unlike the years of fame and gossip, of historic drinking in the evenings of illusory luxuries and waste. Pivano lists some of the serious blows taken by Fitzgerald in the transition from the late 1920s to the late 1930s: the epochal passage of '29, his wife's illness, debts, TBC, heart disease, the failure of *Tender is the Night*, Hollywood failure,

---

9　Among the enormous quantity of texts on cinema, at least three titles are worth mentioning. For an in-depth history and among the best see G. Rondolino, *Storia del cinema*, UTET, Turin 1995. On the cinema of the U.S.A., we refer to M. De Benedictis, *Il cinema americano. Dalle origini ai giorni nostri*, Newton Compton, Rome 2005. A very acute and original text on film language is that of Lucilla Albano, *La caverna dei giganti. Scritti sull'evoluzione del dispositivo cinematografico*, Pratiche Editrice, Turin 1992.

10　F. Pivano, *Prefazione a Gli ultimi fuochi* di Francis Scott Fitzgerald, Mondadori, Milan 1952, p. 5.

and alcohol into whose maelstrom he throws himself almost as a slow premeditated suicide.

Yet, that Fitzgerald is not in tune with the new decade (the last one he has to live through) is absolutely not true. Just read the last novel, *The Last Fires*, with the tycoon Monroe Star, who shows that he understands very well where the States are going, the film industry, the crazy fun times that are now behind him, the sense of remorse worthy of an end of the *Belle Époque*.[11]

Italian critics summarise the turning point of 1929 thus well:

> during the depression there were no nice, handsome students, during the depression there were no good jazz songs; after the depression the rich no longer knew how to be happy in public, after the depression people spoke with banal vulgarity; after the depression people no longer got joyously drunk at parties.[12]

---

11   It should be remembered that the Anglo-Saxons distinguish the novel as a narrative inspired by reality, from the fantasy-type *romance*. On these two genres we refer to the profound reflections of two of the greatest American literati of the 20th century, Bloom and Frye: "the American prose *romance* has been exalted as a genre, which has helped to make Faulkner, Hemingway and Fitzgerald our foremost writers of prose *fiction* of the 20th century (...) The effect of this exaltation of *romance* above the 'realistic' novel has been that visionary narratives such as Faulkner's *As I Lay Dying* (...) Thomas Pynchon's *The Crying of Lot 49* have enjoyed greater critical esteem than (...) *An American Tragedy* by Theodor Dreiser. Currently, a new revision of genres has begun with the rise of the journalistic novel, such as Truman Capote's *In Cold Blood* (...) *An American Tragedy* has regained much of its lustre in the atmosphere of such works'. H. Bloom, *The Western Canon. The Books and School of the Ages*, Bompiani, Milan 1996, p. 18. "Romance is of all literary forms the one that comes closest to representing the dream or satisfaction of human desires, and thus has a strangely paradoxical function from a social point of view. In every age, the dominant social or intellectual class tends to project its ideals into some form of romance in which the virtuous heroes and beautiful heroines represent the ideals, and the villains the threat (...). And yet in romance there is a genuinely "proletarian" element that is never satisfied by its various incarnations, and indeed the incarnations themselves indicate that however great a change takes place in society, romance will appear again, more insatiable than ever, looking for new hopes and new desires on which to feed." N. Frye, *Anatomia della critica. Quattro saggi*, Einaudi, Turin 1969, p. 247.

12   Pivano, *Prefazione...*, cit., pp. 15-16. Again by Pivano, see at least other two works: the illuminating essay *L'"età del jazz".. Prefazione a Belli e dannati* by Francis Scott Fitzgerald, Mondadori, Milan 1954 and the volume *Amici*

To represent the distance between the myth of strength and adventure in Hemingway and the myth of beautiful, rich, short, and damnable youth in Fitzgerald, consider a real-life dialogue between the two. The latter says to the former: 'You know, Ernst, the rich are, how shall we say.... different'. And the other replies: 'Yes, Scott, they have more money'.[13]

But it would be wrong to think that the author of *The Beautiful and Damned* is unaware of what is happening before his eyes and of the illusory myth he himself incarnates. The characters in the novels are young people immersed in the languor of painful, sometimes unrequited loves (echoes of the initial rejection received by Zelda, before the success of *This Side of Paradise*); as well as lost in the exalting of stock market speculations, insane gains and equally insane losses, sudden ruin, and consequent suicides. Corruption is very much present in the pages of Fitzgerald: corruption of money, of government, of faces and bodies, under make-up and the bob hair of the tomboys (the so-called flappers), the long mouthpieces for scandalous smoking and the exhilarating rides in Packard or De Soto convertibles.[14]

Let's hear more from Pivano about the maturation of Fitzgerald's social analysis in *The Last Tycoon*:

---

  scrittori. Quarant'anni di incontri e scoperte con gli autori americani, Mondadori, Milan 1995.

13 An example of Fitzgerald's critical acuity, also concerning his friend Hemingway, can be found in the essay *How to Waste Material: A Note on My Generation*, in F.S. Fitzgerald, *Crepuscolo di uno scrittore*, Mondadori, Milan 1992, pp. 199-207.

14 The philosopher Givone speaks of 'everyday life consigned to the fable' about don Quijote, the unwitting (?) founder of the modern novel. But also, Jay Gatsby in *The Great Gatsby*, Monroe Star in *The Last Tycoon*, Anthony Patch in *The Beautiful and Damned*, Dick Diver in *Tender is the Night*, as well as Amory Blaine in *This Side of Paradise*, are all protagonists for whom the double meaning between *fabula* and reality applies. And so, the circle continues, from Cervantes to Fitzgerald, to the present day: "A kind of double meaning confuses the protagonist of what can be considered the first modern novel. (...) that the everyday is consigned to the fable. And thus, freed from banality and insignificance, since the fable is truer than the truth." S. Givone, *Dire le emozioni. La costruzione dell'interiorità nel romanzo moderno*, in Moretti (ed.), *Il romanzo...*, cit., p. 377. The reference is obviously to don Quijote.

The protagonists of the story are typical American money hunters, and their victim is a typical Fitzgeraldian character for whom wealth is but an illusion of youth and youth is but a dream; but important in the unfolding of the events is Fitzgerald's precise indictment of the corruption inherent in wealth. (...) in novels that are not fantasy and they make the same accusation, the happy ending is not there, and the great Gatsby dies a corpse, the doctor in *Tender is the Night* ends up disintegrated and the heiress in *The Beautiful and Damned* ends up paralysed and disfigured by his own lust.[15]

____

15   Pivano, *Introduzione...*, cit., p. 7.

3
THE ART OF BECOMING A MYTH.
ERNEST HEMINGWAY

3.1 *A sublimated autobiography*

Hemingway had clear ideas about his work. For him, the writer had to be true to life, his invention born of life experience and be authentic. In stories, it was necessary to create 'living people, not characters', figures coming directly from one's own experience, one's own heart, one's own culture, while maintaining absolute fidelity to the facts. If a prose writer was able to write with enough truth, the reader would be able to perceive his world, even if the author only talked about a small part of it, like when you look at an iceberg and, even though you only see an eighth of it, you still feel its size.[1] If, therefore, Hemingway had set himself the rule of not 'inventing' anything, the close link between his life and his fiction is evident. In fact, he chose to recount episodes related to his personal experiences and did so in an almost concealed manner at first, but, with time, in an increasingly publicized manner. This chronicle of his own adventures ended up constituting a sort of 'sublimated autobiography' over time.[2] But was Hemingway really a brave soldier, an infallible hunter, a heroic war correspondent, a swashbuckling bullfighter, a lonely navigator in the ocean waves? Not even the naivest doubt today that one should take his 'accounts' with the benefit of inventory.

Of course, the discrepancy between reality and fiction in his books is not relevant to the evaluation of the work. However, one cannot fail to notice the discrepancy between this appeal to truth and

---

1   E. Hemingway, *Morte nel pomeriggio*, Mondadori, Milan 1961, pp. 163-164.
2   E. Romano (ed.), *Album Hemingway*, Mondadori, Milan 1988, *Introduzione* by M. D. Amico, p. VII.

his tendency to mould an idealised character that was to become the public image of himself. It is precisely this ability to create his myth, that legend that he was able to impose himself on the imagination of millions of readers, which constitutes one of his masterpieces,[3] but also the root of his tragic fate.

Ernest Miller Hemingway was born on 21 July 1899 in Oak Park (Chicago) to Clarence Edmonds Hemingway, an idealistic and wealthy doctor who had chosen to live with his family in that wooded area of Michigan. Physically he was as massive as his son would have been and loved the outdoors, hunting, fishing, stuffed animals and field cooking, all passions he would pass on to Ernest. He soon took him with him on his raids through woods and rivers, teaching him how to handle weapons and tools. All of this enters the boy's imagination, imbues him, so much so that it becomes material for stories told to relatives and friends, with good doses of inventiveness.[4]

His mother had been an opera singer and would have liked to initiate her son into the world of music and art, but Ernest preferred boxing, swimming and life in the open air, in that quiet town where there were - apart from work - only two possible activities: church or the bar. Perhaps that was why, in 1917, the young man decided to move to Kansas City. An uncle got him a job as a reporter at the 'Star', a respectable newspaper, which is still important today. He is given the crime beat and so Ernest goes in search of news in hospitals and police stations, moving through a city that was then expanding, a place where the memory of the Frontier was still alive and where crime, cynicism and debauchery were still in the air. Twelfth Street was left to prostitution and was the young reporter's deprived workplace. With his boyish face, he moved between seedy clubs and brothels, without losing himself in that life, but keeping a cautious distance, just enough to observe it.

All of Hemingway's biographers emphasise at this point in his story the importance for the writer of this experience of working in a newspaper. At the 'Star' they gave him a manual of rules for aspiring

---

3   G. Fink - M. Maffi - F. Minganti - B. Tarozzi, *Storia della letteratura americana*, Sansoni, Milan 2001, pp. 256-257.
4   A. Burgess, *Hemingway*, Editrice Nuova, Milan 1983, pp. 11-31.

journalists, which says among other things: 'Use short sentences. Use short first paragraphs. Use energetic language. Be positive, not negative'.[5] These are clearly recognisable elements in what was to become his style as a novelist. Hemingway was in fact confronted with the tradition of Victorian eloquence, with its aestheticism, moralism, and neo-Gothic embellishments, the structure with intricate subordinate sentences, the heavy allusions. That is why he soon felt he wanted to break away from those limits, to search for a prose that was dry, made up of unspoken words, attentive to the observation of gestures and environments, as in a photograph that would allow the restlessness of life to be perceived. There was to be no rhetoric, no mannered lyricism, only truth and simplicity, at least in appearance. His rough and poor prose was in fact the result of complex work, of the Flaubertian search for the right word, a search that was, however, mimicked by a certain American ruggedness, a non-superficial irony and skilful stylistic research. This is certainly the lesson of journalism, later filtered through the artist's elaboration. The path, however, was to take a few more years to reach maturity, also passing through a world war.

Ted Brumback, a colleague of Hemingway's, had spent four months driving ambulances in France, an experience that fascinated young Ernest. It does not take him long to quit his job and leave for Europe. He is part of the Red Cross, has his nice uniform and soon the myth of the warrior writer spreads, even though he never actually fought in any war.

He arrived in Milan in the summer of 1918 and immediately had to intervene in clearing injured people in a bombed-out factory. The impact with the conflict is hard, an experience of horror that is difficult to forget. However, Ernest wants to experience life in the trenches at first hand and asks to work on the Piave front. Caporetto is far away, the war has already taken a clear victory turn for Italy and the Entente, but the fighting continues. On 8 July, while distributing foodstuffs to soldiers, an Austrian Minewerfer explodes nearby, killing one man and wounding another. Hemingway loads

---

5   N. Pivano, *Cronologia*, in E. Hemingway, *Romanzi*, edited by F. Pivano, Mondadori, Milan 1992, vol. I, p. XL.

him onto his shoulders and tries to carry him to safety, but is in turn hit by a machine gun discharge. He is soon rescued and transferred to the American military hospital in Milan, where he experiences treatment quite different from that of soldiers engaged in the conflict. At the facility, 18 nurses treat four patients. Ernest's wound is serious, but not severe. He writes enthusiastically to his parents a few weeks later:

> The machine gun bullet felt like an icy snowball hitting my leg. However, it knocked me to the ground. I got back on my feet and took my wounded man to the emergency room. There I collapsed. The Italian I had with me had got blood all over my jacket and it looked like someone had put jam in my trousers and then drilled holes to make it splash out. The captain who was there was a friend of mine. It was his trench and he said, "Poor Hem. He'll be R.I.P. soon." That is, Rest in Peace. They thought I had been hit in the chest, because of the jacket all covered in blood. However, I had it taken off along with the shirt. Underneath I had no shirt, and the old torso was intact. Then they said I'd probably make it.[6]

For Hemingway, the war is already over. Now all he has left is a flirtation with Agnes von Kurowski, one of the nurses in the American hospital with whom he falls in love without really being reciprocated, and the glory of returning to the country. The young man, in fact, is the first American soldier wounded in Italy. Before him, only the unfortunate Lieutenant Edward McKey had been wounded, but he was killed, a story that was not very popular with the American public. Much better was the story of the young and dashing Hemingway, heroic and, above all, a survivor, an example of American valour in Europe.

On his return home, after the hangover of celebrations and fame, Ernest realises that he has fallen ill with love for the old continent. He no longer wants to talk about his country, nor to be a chronicler. Now he wants to write stories, to talk about the world he has encountered, so infinitely richer than the one he came from. He

---

6   Letter from E. Hemingway to his parents, Milan 18 August 1918, in E. Hemingway - A. Von Kurowski, *In amore e in guerra*, Mursia, Milan 1992, p. 188.

finds a small job for the 'Toronto Star', marries Elizabeth Hadley Richardson who has a modest income and, with her, leaves for Paris. They arrive there in the autumn of 1921 and immediately enter the circle of Americans transplanted in France: Ezra Pound, Gertrude Stein, Scott Fitzgerlad, John Dos Passos, Sylvia Beach.

The Hemingways are not doing very well, but Ernest can write. He starts a collaboration with Ford Madox Ford, working on his magazine 'Transatlantic Review' and, above all, preparing short stories, under the guidance of Ezra Pound and Gertrud Stein, whom he considers his masters. In the meantime, he managed to publish Three Stories and Ten Poems (1923) and In Our Time (1925), the latter with Scribner, the publisher who was to accompany him all his life, together with the precious editor Maxwell Perkins. The waters begin to move, although success has not yet arrived. For this, perhaps, a novel is needed, although Hemingway was an author who never set out to write one. He preferred the measure of the short story and, only if he realised that the story tended to expand, would he start thinking about it, letting it grow without opposition. This happened to him for the first time in Spain.

He had been there a first time to watch the bullfight and returned in 1925 with his wife - whom he soon left for Pauline Pfeiffer, although they had a son - and a group of friends, Harold Loeb, Bill Smith, Pat Guthrie and his companion, Lady Duff Twysten, the personification of glamour and seduction. The group wants to attend the San Firmin festival in Pamplona, where the star is the 19-year-old bullfighter Cayetano Odoñez.

Despite the eve's enthusiasm, the holiday turns out to be very tense, there are tensions, quarrels, misunderstandings that generate in Hemingway a tangle of emotions, guilt, animosity, vagueness. All this has to find its catharsis and becomes the material for *The Sun Also Rises* (also published under the title *Fiesta*). Thus, Harlod Loeb becomes Robert Cohn, Lady Duff turns into Lady Brett and Hemingway into Jake Barnes. These characters spend a life as alcoholics, first in Paris and then in Pamplona, where they are involved in the regenerating ritual of bullfighting. Barnes' character is powerless because of a war wound, living this half-life, aware of the barrenness of his loveless existence. Salvation can only depend on sacrifice, on a ritual in which blood flows. The confrontation between man and bull can decide the confrontation with death itself and, in a certain sense, dominate it.[7]

The book was a great success with the public and critics. At not even thirty years of age, Hemingway has already arrived. Now he can be a full- time man of action, transporting his life in a series of wonderful books, in which everything is transfigured into the image of a self that is not the public or even the real self, but what he wants others to see. It is the beginning of the creation of his myth.

The passage is also punctuated by biographical elements. The marriage to his new wife Pauline, his first child with her, the move to Key West, where the writer encounters the wonder of the ocean, the new frontier for his adventures. There is also the dramatic suicide of his father, who shoots himself in 1928, throwing the responsibility for the family onto Ernest, but generating in him a profound sense of shame, as if the gesture were a sign of great cowardice, of an inability to dominate life. However, the time had come for Hemingway to release the material of experiences and images stored during the First World War.

A Farewell to Arms came out in 1929, along with many other masterpieces dedicated to war - such as Remarque's *All Quiet on the Western Front* - right at the beginning of the great crisis that was about to hit the United States and Europe, but nothing seemed to be able to stop the writer's great success. The book is immediately loved, it is immediately bought by Hollywood, which will make a bad film of it with Gary Cooper, changing its final, much to the author's disappointment. The story is the mythical one of a self-styled Frederic Henry who is a real fighter and participates in the retreat of Caporetto and is wounded. In fiction, the love between him and the nurse blossoms, so much so that it drives the soldier to desertion in Switzerland, but everything is shattered by the girl's death in childbirth.

Despite his great success and the lightness with which he seems to be able to churn out masterpieces, Hemingway becomes increasingly edgy, arrogant, pre-powerful, even ungrateful towards those who

---

7   Burgess, *Hemingway...*, cit., p. 77.

have helped him over the years. He also begins to drink excessively and his relationship with Pauline sours. By her, meanwhile, he has had a second child. The couple dreams of a safari in Africa, where they can experience big game hunting and the adventure of months spent on the savannah. For Hemingway, it is about putting his philosophy of heroism into practice. By now, the United States is too friendly a territory, bullfighting is not enough because he is not the one to measure himself against, the First World War is water under the bridge. He needs a new arena in which to challenge himself and the self-image he wants to give the world. Nothing can open up these horizons better than Africa.

They manage to leave at the end of 1933 for Kenya. They are led by the white hunter Philip Percival, affable, bold, the protagonist of many fine hunting stories. The writer immediately gets on well with him and manages to do himself credit, capturing his lion and many other dangerous animals. Of all these, he will have trophies made for his Key West home. *Green Hills of Africa* (1935) is the account of this experience. Death is treated less dramatically here than in earlier works. The author's interest seems to be to treat it light-heartedly, in almost sporting code terms. Hemingway presents himself with the characteristics of the great hunter, with rifle at his side, strength, courage, concerned to show all his virility on every page. This is an element that will also appear in his later works, although it is a trait that does little to match genuine virility.

In the meantime, war breaks out in Spain, a suitable theatre for a writer who wants to experience first-hand the experiences to be recounted in his books, a new chance to measure himself against his myth. With Pauline, the story is now over and Martha Fischer Gellhorn, with her shiny shoulder-length blond hair and the grace of a film star, but also a writer and journalist, opposed to fascism, like Hemingway, is already appearing in his life. For him, choosing a political position in Spain is difficult because, given his life choices, he cannot easily espouse the cause of the National Front. However, it is precisely in his aversion to totalitarian systems that he finds a coherent position.

He reaches Spain with his new partner and the assignment from the North American Newspaper Alliance to report on the conflict.

Hemingway travels far and wide, sees cities and fighters, but his pieces are not appreciated by the newspapers. The editors would like news articles, in which facts, concrete information, explanations of what is happening are given, while the writer only talks about himself, tells impressionistic stories in which he is the only protagonist. The experience soon came to an end and his contribution to the Republican cause was limited to a few public speeches in the United States. Hemingway retires to Cuba, to the Finca Vigía, where he can watch the cockfights, write without interruption and, in less than an hour, be out to sea fishing for marlin with his boat, the Pilar.

3.2 *The prison of myth*

The Finca Vigía, also known as the Guardia Farm, was an enclave of wealth and order in an area of poor and dilapidated Cuban villages and towns. The property had five hectares of garden, a pasture for cows, a vegetable garden, an orchard, and large plants. There was a pleasant guest annexe and a square tower that Hemingway used to retire to write in peace, although it was frequented mainly by the thirty cats of the house. There were ten servants: three gardeners, a chauffeur, a waiter, a Chinese cook, a carpenter, two housekeepers and a man in charge of breeding the fighting cocks. On the gate at the edge of the property, two signs in English and Spanish invited visitors to come by appointment only.

After his divorce with Pauline, Hemingway had bought the Finca Vigía for Martha as a wedding present. The price paid for the estate had been $12,500, a figure derived from the first receipts of the writer's last novel, the one matured in the years following the Spanish War experience. *For Whom the Bell Tolls* was in fact published in 1940 and was a predictable success with the public: sales skyrocketed, the story was immediately bought by Hollywood for a film adaptation, and it was the book of the year in America. However, despite the positive reception, Hemingway perceives that this novel brings him the wrong kind of celebrity. By now, he is no longer the promising young writer with the potential to reinvent the linguistic canon of his era, but he has also failed to become the influential old man of American literature, too bound as he is in his work to action and the myth of himself. The style of the novel is in fact no longer innovative. It merely cashes in on what has gone before. The story, while compelling, of an American fighting in Spain for the Republican forces, his assignment to destroy a bridge and his love for Maria, is unable to become a strong literary work. Hemingway's wartime experience is effectively transposed into the story, but the historical context is presented scholastically, without the strength to really integrate it into the narrative. It is no coincidence that authoritative intellectuals object to this book being awarded the Pulitzer Prize, even though Maria, and especially Pilar, the woman of the partisan leader, are the two most successful female characters in Hemingway's work.

The Second World War, meanwhile, has exploded in Europe with all its drama. The writer and man of action is fatally drawn to it, although his energy is no longer what it was in his twenties. At the beginning of the conflict, he embarks on a mission with the Pilar in Cuban waters as head of a counterespionage organisation, but the affair has more the air of a goliard than of a heroic anti-Nazi endeavour. It does not take long before the American administration withdraws its support for the initiative, and everyone returns home in an orderly fashion. At the Finca Vigía, Hemingway tries to work as hard as he can, but is unable to put together any particularly significant books. He therefore decides to move to the theatre of war, working as a war correspondent, as he has already done in other circumstances.

In 1944, he arrived in London, to later join the Normandy landings following the Allied army in Europe. For seven months, he will follow the troops through the France to be liberated, at the regiment of Colonel Charles Trueman Lanham, who will remain one of his military heroes. He also found a way to join a group of French partisans, even taking command of them and passing information to the Allied forces, until he reached Paris in the days of liberation. The French passage will also bring him a new relationship with Mary Welsh, who will become his fourth and final wife.

However, the Second World War is the last great event. His powerful physique, his energy, his great vitality, begin to take a toll. Hemingway suffers from severe migraines, hypertension, and his liver condition continues to be uncomfortable. So he devotes himself to pleasant trips, such as the one to Italy that will last a long time, and to retreats at the Finca Vigía where he tries to write a new masterpiece to revitalise himself a little, at a time when his myth seems to be dimming and even his most loyal admirers begin to fear that his vein has run out.

After *For Whom the Bell Tolls*, he did not publish anything else of significance. The book *Across the River and Into the Trees*, which came about following his trip to Italy, is an important work for him. It is overshadowed by the presence of the young Adriana Ivancich, who has been at his side for some time, not as a companion, but as a daughter. It is she who inspires him the character of Renata, the beautiful countess in love with the old soldier who will die of a heart attack, despite that precious presence. Critics harshly rejected the novel, pointing out the lack of balance, the improper use of many images, the writing not up to the great author's standards. As often happens in life, however, the most difficult moments are actually turning points that can lead to unexpected successes.

Hemingway reacts to defeat with work. Holed up at the Finca Vigìa, he strives to produce a great book about the sea. The text will only come out posthumously under the title *Islands in the Strean*. At the moment, he finds himself holding too much material, a long and monotonous piece of writing to which he still cannot give strength. He then detaches a core from it, works on it and begins to describe the story of an old Cuban fisherman who ventures into the middle of the ocean in his little boat for days on the trail of a large marlin. After a long struggle, he manages to catch it, but on his way back to the miserable village where he lives, he is attacked by sharks that devour his prey. When he docks all that remains of his booty is the carcass. The old man embodies courage in the face of failure, he does not care about the danger of being killed, even though he knows that one of him and the fish will have to die. The final outcome of the story, the fisherman's defeat by the adverse forces of nature, leaves his honour intact, however, because Santiago did not really fail. He has maintained the right pride and humility. *The Old Man and the Sea* was published in a special issue of 'Life' in September 1952. In just 48 hours, the magazine sold 5,318,650 copies. The following year, the novel was awarded the Pulitzer Prize and, in 1954, Hemingway was awarded the Nobel Prize. However, he cannot travel to Stockholm, as he is still convalescing from a serious plane crash in Africa. His physical health is permanently compromised. The problems in his body soon lead to severe states of depression, which result in the writer no longer being able to work. A severe mania for persecution begins to grow in him. He is convinced that he is being spied on or followed, that he is in danger from plots hatched against him. He begins to behave strangely, has continuous crying fits.

In the shadows of those moments, a small light is shed by the chance discovery at the Ritz in Paris, a hotel assiduously frequented by the writer, of a crate containing manuscripts that belonged to him and were going up in the late 1920s. These are materials from which he was able, despite his condition, to draw his last work, *A Moveable Feast*, the story of the life and characters of his youthful years in Paris.

Hemingway has meanwhile had to leave the Finca Vigía. The Cuban revolution made his stay on the island unsafe, at least in his perception. He therefore spent a lot of time in Idaho, in Ketchum, where he owned a villa in the mountains. The house is on two floors, with a large terrace and large windows. The writer spends terrible days there, obsessed by his fears, increasingly weak, abandoned by his body and confused in his thoughts. He finally decides to seek medical treatment for his liver problems and high blood pressure, but the worst problem is depression. His wife has found him several times with a rifle in his hand. A psychiatrist, Dr. Rome, recommends a series of electroshock treatments. The aim is to alleviate the symptoms of his malaise and, at the same time, to erase part of his memory, in the belief that, by eliminating the memories, the traumas from which the depression started would also disappear.

The consequences of the therapy, however, are devastating. Hemingway suffers from aphasia and sees his memory compromised, the gift that had been his greatest asset throughout his life, with the extraordinary ability to store images and remember details, an immense and wonderful material with which to build his stories.

Betrayed by his body and his own mind, the writer feels he no longer possesses anything. The final decline is swift and horrible.

Hemingway loses his strength completely, loses weight, cries, can no longer even answer letters. He decided to commit suicide with a shotgun blast on 2 July 1961, at the age of 62. Long before, when he was still hospitalised in Milan due to his wound in the First World War, he had written to his parents in a letter: 'How much better it is to die in the happy time of youth yet to be disillusioned, to go out in a blaze of light, than to see oneself worn out in the body and with shattered illusions'.[8] Not even twenty years old, he already seemed to have glimpsed his own destiny.

---

8   Letter from E. Hemingway to his parents, Milan 18 October 1918, in Hemingway - Von Kurowski, *In amore...*, cit., p. 197.

4
THE LORD OF YOKNAPATAWPHA.
WILLIAM FAULKNER

4.1 *That 'stamp of homeland'*

Yoknapatawpha County lies seventy-five miles south of Memphis in the North Mississippi Delta. The land is red clay, eroded, and forms an enclosed countryside, where one encounters plantations, old homesteads, cemeteries, swamps, and the great river, sometimes quiet and silent, sometimes turbulent and wild. Two dusty roads intersect, forming a cross, in Jefferson, the centre of the county. In the town are the jail, the town hall square, the Beat Four, the old mansion called Old Frenchman's Place and the railway. The tracks run north-south, parallel to the main road to Memphis Junction. The territory is 2,400 square miles and is home to a population of 15,611 in 1936, of which 6,298 were white and 9,313 were black.

Many are the generations that have inhabited this land over time: native Indians, slaves, plantation owners, old and noble ladies, but also soldiers of the Civil War - and later the First World War - guerrilla fighters in the bush, preachers, lawyers, judges, students, farmers, traders, exploiters, smugglers, murderers. They all carry a burden of guilt, the legacy of the slave period. Everything in Yoknapatawpha County - including the lives and fate of its inhabitants - has one owner: William Faulkner.

In fact, this mythical region only exists in the writer's books, although behind the fake names are real places - the northern Mississippi, the small town of Oxford ('Jefferson') and Lafayette County ('Yoknapatawpha County') - as well as real-life stories and characters, such as John Sartoris, the protagonist of the novel *Sartoris* (1929), which is based on Faulkner's great-grandfather.

After a phase of thematic and stylistic research, the writer had discovered in this detailed knowledge of people and places the main resource for his fantastic creation. Poking around in this world – that "postage stamp of the homeland' - he managed to overcome a superficial representation of the South as a historical region, to make it the starting point for analysing universal human problems, with an effectiveness that made that fantasy world something absolutely real. Time takes on a very special dimension there. In the Faulknerian imagination it is an element united in a profound way. There is no real distinction between present and past, but both act on things, so much so that reality is what past and present have made of an event or object.[1] And the deep rootedness in this ideal time, a time that can be experienced in some way and that therefore becomes the bearer of profound meanings, is what makes it possible to identify 'eternal truths'. It thus provides the criterion of judgement with which to evaluate the characters and their actions. No contemporary author managed to achieve as much power as Faulkner in creating a real and cohesive world, a world that never ceases to convey the experience of humanity.

William Faulkner was born in New Albany on 25 September 1897. His father, Murray, ran a stud farm and an ironmonger's shop. He was later a business manager at the University of Mississippi based in Oxford, where the family moved in 1902. He was a pragmatic man, worthy heir to the Faulkner tradition, starting with the figure of his grandfather (great- grandfather for the writer), William, a legendary character in the area, colonel of an assault group during the Civil War, a politician, owner of the railway, twice accused of murder and always acquitted. The writer's mother was called Maud Butler. She had a talent for drawing and sculpture, as well as a certain sense of humour that calmed the severity of her father's family. Next to her, there emerged the great figure of Caroline Barr, the black governess called Mummy Callie, the woman who looked after the children and to whom little William became deeply attached. From her voice he heard the stories of the Civil War, of the slaves, of the people of the county, the tales that would later be reworked in his novels. It is no

---

1   F.J. Hoffman, *Faulkner*, Il Castoro, Florence 1967, p. 5 and p. 15.

coincidence that when Mummy died at the age of one hundred in 1940, Faulkner dedicated *Go Down, Moses* to her. At her funeral, he read a funeral oration in which he said, among other things:

> Caroline has been by my side for a lifetime. I consider it a privilege to have accompanied her to the end of hers. After my father's death, it fell to me to represent, in *Mummy*'s eyes, the head of the family to which she had devoted half a century of loyalty and devotion. But the relationship between us has never turned into that between master and servant. She has always remained one of my first memories, not only as a person, but as a source of authority over my conduct and security for my health, and of active and constant affection and love. She has been an active and constant standard of good conduct. From her I learnt to be sincere, to avoid waste, to be considerate of the weak and respectful towards the elderly. I saw loyalty to a family that was not hers, devotion and love for people she did not beget. [...] If there is a heaven, she has gone there.[2]

As a boy, the young Faulkner explores the region around his small town, he is fascinated by the woods, the river, the hunting, but what attracts him most are the people, the street people, the clever and the profiteers, the Civil War veterans. Meanwhile, his friend Phil Stone, the son of a banker, makes him read the important authors of his era, from Ezra Pound to Sherwood Anderson. With Phil he embarks on small adventures, until he decides to abandon his studies before graduating. He attempts to participate in the First World War, enlisting in the Royal Flying Corps in Toronto,[3] but is discharged before leaving because by the time he finishes his training, the conflict is already over. By the time he returns home, Faulkner has decided to devote himself to writing, while his father only wishes to find him a serious job. To humour him, he embarks on various odd jobs, until he leaves everything to go to New Orleans, where he becomes friends with Sherwood Anderson and begins to publish short stories in magazines.

---

2   W. Faulkner, *W.F. Scritti, discorsi e lettere*, edited by J.B. Meriwether, Il Saggiatore, Milan 2010, pp. 139-140.
3   Letter from W. Faulkner to his mother, New Haven, 7 June 1918, in W. Faulkner, *Pensando a casa. Lettere alla madre e al padre*, edited by J.G. Watson, Rosellina Archinto, Milan 1993, pp. 11-12.

Critics tend to divide Faulkner's work into three periods: the apprenticeship period (1924-29), during which he tried to figure out what kind of writer to become and what themes to tackle; the 'genius period' (1929-36), in which he succeeded in producing 'the most remarkable series of novels ever written by a single person in such a short period of time'[4]; and the consolidation and affirmation phase (1940 to his death).

In the first part of his literary career, which took place between New Orleans, Oxford, and a short trip to Europe, Faulkner produced only three works: *The Marble Faun* (1924), a collection of poems with ample echoes of late 19th century mannerism, and the novels *Soldier's Pay* (1926) and *Mosquitoes* (1927). The first book was published with the help of Sherwood Anderson and tells of a soldier returning horribly wounded from the First World War. Around the figure of the dying man, many presences alternate - his father, his fiancée, a soldier, a widow - and each one is illuminated in the confrontation with the truth of which the doomed hero is the bearer. Instead, *Mosquitoes* has a satirical tone, imitating some of Huxley's novels, and is about a reception on a yacht off the coast of New Orleans. A rich lady has gathered a wide assortment of guests for the party. Among them is the woman's niece who escapes with the stewart, but is attacked by mosquitoes and is forced to return to the yacht. Despite some positive reading by the critics of the time, these works disappeared in the face of the writer's later works, like when Faulkner decided to set his sights on his own land.

The moment of transition is marked by *Sartoris* (1929), the novel in which the Faulkner family legend is uncritically dealt with, starting from the time of the great-grandfather and ending with that of the writer himself. The young aviator Bayard Sartoris, a World War I veteran, is haunted by the death of his brother who fell in battle. To deal with his guilt, he throws himself into reckless ventures, until he dies testing a new aircraft. The central theme of the book is the young Sartoris' confrontation with previous generations of his family, with the history in which the roots of his own war lie. This book projects Faulkner directly into Yoknapatawpha County and somehow reveals

---

4   Hoffman, *Faulkner...*, cit., p. 6.

to him the perspective that his work must take. His language, his style, which on the one hand brings dialects and slang expressions to the surface, and on the other hand relies on European expressive techniques, especially Joyce's stream of consciousness, also begins to take shape here.[5]

The 'period of genius' thus began with *Sartoris*, but saw the succession of an impressive string of important works: *The Sound and the Fury* (1929), *As I Lay Dying* (1930), *Sanctuary* (1931), *Light in August* (1932), *Absalom, Absalom!* (1936). These are all works of the highest literary level, in which Faulkner manages to fully unleash his language and create complex narrative architectures. *The Sound and the Fury*, for instance, is the story of lost innocence and a family turned in on itself. The dramatic tale of Caddy's relationship with Dalton Ames - a betrayal of morality and tradition - is entrusted to four overlapping voices, four narrators each speaking with their own images, style, narrative sequences, and points of view. This technique is even more pronounced in *As I Lay Dying*. The story of Addie Brunden, who, dying, asks relatives to be buried in Jefferson and the journey through a thousand difficulties is reported from no less than fifteen different points of view. The voices are those of family members, divided into fifty-nine narrative sequences. Each character carries the action and reflects on what it means to him or her. The novel proves to be a psychological study of numerous perspectives on a truth, that of being born and living.

Sanctuary is Faulkner's most commercial book and, of these, perhaps his least powerful. The novel examines the failure of the law - of legal ethics, of moral force - of a 'lawyer of goodwill', Horace Benbow, who cannot find a reason for boundless evil, embodied by the figure of a thug called Popeye, and is therefore unable to oppose him.

Much more intense is *Light in August*. The book presents an important element characterising the mentality of the US South, the rigid ethics of Protestantism, which elevates duty above charity. The 'ret- titude' then proves incapable of forgiving human weakness and

---

5   F. Pivano, *Pagine americane*, Frassinelli, Milan 2005, pp. 1415-1416.

can even lead, as in the novel, to the lynching of a person, in the story to that of Joe Christmas.

Absalom, Absalom!, the last in chronological order, is the mainstay of the Yoknapatawpha tales. It tells the story of a man who, humiliated as a child by a black servant in livery, is seized by a need for power and domination over others. Thomas Sutpen is willing to sacrifice everything to this ambition, even his humanity, and for this he is destined for inevitable defeat. In this book, Faulkner re-examines the cultural context of the South and endeavours to analyse its effects on those who inhabit it and live that mentality. Almost none of the characters can really understand it, many hate it, but all must adapt to it.

This group of books, published in the short space of a few years, from 1929 to 1936, is considered by many scholars to be unparalleled in contemporary American literature.

4.2 *On the side of the good guys*

As everyone who writes well knows, being able to produce important literary works and be appreciated by critics is often not enough to guarantee sufficient income to lead a quiet life. Faulkner knew this well, too, who for years had to tighten his belt and muddle through as best he could. In 1929, he had moved in with Estelle Oldham, who had just returned from a previous marriage, which brought him in dowry two still young children. Their relationship soon proved rather difficult. Both were addicted to alcohol abuse, confronted with a difficult financial situation, and even faced a suicide attempt by Estelle. The writer tried to get out of the impasse by producing a novel 'with the specific intention of making money'.[6] He published, in fact, but came too little.

He then conceived a story that, in his intentions, should have allowed him to burn a print run of at least 10,000 copies. The first draft of the novel was rejected by the publisher who was scandalised. Faulkner then revised it and the book saw the light

---

6   W. Faulkner, *W.F. Scritti, discorsi...*, cit., p. 197.

of day. It was about *Sanctuary* and was unanimously condemned from the first appearance as 'scandalous', "chock-full of sadistic cruelty", unnecessarily "horrific and morbid".[7] The story was about a schoolgirl from a good family, Temple Drake, who by chance ends up in Popeye's clandestine distillery. The criminal kills a man in front of the girl and rapes her with a cob. Not content with this abuse, he sets her up in a house of prostitution and arranges for a young man named Red to become her lover to witness their sexual encounters. Popeye is in fact impotent.

Despite the criticism and the Great Depression, the book sold well and was indeed the most 'commercial' of Faulkner's works. However, it did not solve the financial problems of the writer, who had meanwhile experienced a terrible loss. His first child, Alabama, was born prematurely and died a few days after birth. Instead, in 1933, Jill, who would remain his only child, was born.

Like other authors of his generation, Faulkner managed to find an important source of income from working for Hollywood. For several years, he had occasional contracts for scripts and screenplays, most of which never became films. He also spent periods in California, alone or with his family, although his base remained the small town of Oxford. During this period, the problem of alcoholism also worsened, so much so that in 1936 he even had to go into detoxification treatment. However, his fame grew, the contracts became more attractive, and the financial situation seemed less haunting than it had been in the past. Faulkner had now reached his maturity as an author. The third phase of his career was opening up, that of consolidation and definitive fulfilment.

The books of this period can be grouped into a few strands: the saga of the Snopes, comprising *The Hamlet* (1940), *The Town* (1957) and *The Mansion* (1959); the writings specifically about blacks, considered as a race, an ethnic group and a moral problem - *Go Down, Moses* and *Intruder in the Dust* - and the works in which Faulkner tried to clearly expound and deal with the theme of 'eternal truths', the faith that man must not lose. In these novels, Faulkner relied on a kind of moral spokesperson, who sometimes

---

7   Hoffman, *Faulkner...*, cit., p. 56.

speaks almost on behalf of his author, Gave Stevens, (*Intruder in the Dust, Knight's Gambit, Requiem for a Nun*), or he took the path of a complex allegory that resulted in *A Fable* (1954).[8] However, his works continued to sell poorly, and publishers were unhappy. In the mid-1940s, of his seventeen books, only two were available for consultation at the New York Public Library. Faulkner seems to have fallen into oblivion. Therefore, when he was contacted by Malcolm Cowley, literary editor of 'The New Republic', he was delighted with his proposal to dedicate a long biographical article to him. The writer had always struggled to keep his private life private, but he well understood the importance of an operation to re-evaluate his work.

Cowley's lengthy study was published between 1944 and 1945 in a magazine, attracting a certain amount of attention to Faulkner that the Viking Press proposed to the journalist to edit a paperback anthology of Faulkner's work, although it did not promise to sell as much as Hemingway's *Portable*, which sold 30,000 copies. However, the potential of this collection was clear for all to see, especially since the writer was highly regarded in Europe, indeed, many considered him to be one of the greatest contemporary authors. Sartre, for example, wrote an essay in which he recounted Faulkner's influence on authors such as Camus, de Beauvoir and himself, even stating that young Europeans considered him a 'genius'.[9]

The eve's expectations are fulfilled. *The Portable Faulkner*, released in 1946, provoked worldwide popularity for the writer and revived reprints of out-of-print titles. He was called to the University of Mississippi to give seminars, he began to be invited to the salons that counted, interview requests rained in from all sides and the America Academy of Arts and Letters elected him as one of its members. In the meantime, the novel *Intruder in the Dust* is sold for $50,000 to Metro Goldwyn Mayer, finally beginning the longed-for economic security. However, the ride to worldwide fame has only just begun.

---

8   Ibid, p. 8.
9   F. Pivano, *Cronologia*, in W. Faulkner, *Opere scelte*, edited by F. Pivano, Mondadori, Milan 1995-2004, vol. I, pp. LXXVIII-LXXIX.

In November 1950 Faulkner is in a field near his home. He is fertilising it and preparing it for winter. He is met by a newspaperman, the New York correspondent of a Swedish newspaper, who announces that he has been awarded the Nobel Prize. The writer is in disbelief, as is the town of Oxford, which had not realised Faulkner's great authorial importance. At first, he does not even want to make the trip overseas to Stockholm, because he shuns worldly occasions and, above all, has a persistent alcohol problem. He only agrees after the insistence of many friends, his wife Estelle, and his daughter Jill, who accompanies him to the ceremony. Flying over the Atlantic, he writes the acceptance speech that will remain one of the most appreciated ever delivered in that prestigious venue:

> I feel that the true recipient of this prize is not me as a man, but my work - the work of a lifetime in the agony and sweat of the human spirit, not for glory, let alone profit, but to create out of the materials of the human spirit something that did not exist before. Therefore, I am the simple custodian of this prize. [...] Our tragedy today is a general and universal concrete fear that is so prolonged that we can hardly bear it. There are no longer any problems of the spirit. There is only the question: When will I be blown up? For this reason, the young man or woman writing today forgets the problems of the human heart in conflict with itself, the only ones that can make good writing because they alone are worthy of being told [...]: love and honour and pity and pride and compassion and sacrifice. [The writer] until he learns all this again, will write as if he witnesses the end of man and participates in it. [...] Man will not be content to resist: he will prevail. He is immortal, not because he alone among creatures possesses an unquenchable voice, because he possesses a soul, a spirit capable of compassion and sacrifice and endurance. The duty of the poet, of the writer, is to write about these things. It is his privilege to help man endure [...][10]

Faulkner was the fourth American to receive the honour of the Nobel Prize, but he was the only one to receive almost unanimous critical acclaim. The re-recognition made the writer a public figure with an authority that had not been attributed to him before. He was now at the centre of the literary world, and interviewers no longer

---

10   Faulkner, W.F. *Scritti...*, cit., pp. 142-143.

approached him as in the past to ask him a few questions about his latest book, but solicited him on important topics, hoping to hear high-level reflections.

Faulkner, contrary to what might have been expected, accepted this new role willingly, with a sense of responsibility, almost with emotion towards the importance of the position he was given. He soon took the initiative to critique his own work, to tell about himself and explain everything he had been saying for the past twenty-five years. In this way, he discovered that the man who had written about girls being raped with a corncob, about lynchings, about betrayals, about a filthy, chaotic world full of irrationality and violence, had in fact only intended to defend 'eternal truths'. He was therefore also on the side of the good guys.

These thoughts, expressed effectively in the Stockholm speech, were then rendered dramatically in the complex allegory of A Fable, in which the story of a French corporal is shown in a series of analogies with the life of Christ, to convey an earthly message, namely that man will not only endure adverse fate, but will prevail over it. The book was awarded the Pulitzer Prize in 1955.

Faulkner's life, however, was coming to an end. Alcohol abuse had prostrated his physique, and his mind was beginning to suffer. The writer suffered terrible amnesia, as well as attacks of convulsions and collapses. He had to undergo, as Hemingway had done, electroshock therapy and regular psychiatric treatment, which succeeded in improving his situation. In the meantime, Jill had married, giving him two grandchildren. William Faulkner died in July 1962. The funeral procession passed through Oxford to take the writer's body to the cemetery, taking care, however, to let him first say goodbye one last time to those places that he had been able to fix in his work so effectively.

5
A LOOK THROUGH THE SMOKE.
JOHN STEINBECK

Numerous photographs of John Steinbeck circulate, in the many books about him, on the web and in a thousand other places. In the youthful ones he appears with his square, massive face, imposing nose, large ears, serious but clean-cut gaze, with eyes that look blue, but were actually hazel. He has a moustache, he looks far away, he has almost a certain sweetness in his attitude fixed in the picture. In the photographs of the mature age, however, he has something demonic. A beard has been added, concentrated on the chin, sharp. The big hands with Masonic ring and smoking cigarette, sometimes clasped between the lips to give him an ambiguous expression, between angry and sly. Two very distant image types, not only in time, but in their very message, a duality that has always been structural to the figure of John Steinbeck. A writer, an intellectual who never considered himself as such and always remained a stranger to that world; a great novelist, an author of 'fiction'. And yet one who wanted to see with his own eyes the world he narrated, almost a newspaper reporter; of modest origins, accustomed to living in the still agricultural California countryside and then a citizen of New York; the author of dramatic and comic texts, in a phantasmagoria of different styles and situations; a character impossible to pigeonhole into political categories such as 'left' or 'right'.[1] In his books, he never took a clear stand for one side or the other, trying more to critically show the limits of the different positions. That is why Steinbeck is only Steinbeck.

He was born in Salinas on 27 February 1902. The Californian city, at that times, it was not very populous, two or three thousand

---

1   B. Osimo, *There's no there there*, in J. Steinbeck, *L'America e gli americani e altri scritti*, edited by B. Osimo, Alet Edizioni, Padua 2008, pp. 9-13.

inhabitants perhaps, mostly farmers or employees in a sugar mill. In the writer's recollection, the place was ugly, windswept, and gloomy, like the swamps on which it had originally stood. According to John, Salinas was a place with something of murkiness, a kind of submerged murmur of malice that snaked beneath the surface of that big town not too far from the ocean.

Steinbeck was, however, quite well off there. The family had had economic ups and downs, but was settled and respected. As a boy, after all, John was rather reclusive, an omnivorous reader and already determined to be a writer from high school. He did not, like Hemingway for example, try to stay in the flow of the more avant-garde authors, from Pound to Joyce, but preferred to read everything, even esoteric texts, and was passionate about the events of King Arthur, which conditioned his early works.

He stayed at university for six years, without ever intending to complete it. He went there perhaps to meet his family's expectations, or because he liked listening to some literature lectures. At least one semester was dedicated to work, all kinds of work, including manual labour and hard work. In the meantime, however, he wrote, short stories, a few attempts at a novel.

His first book - *The Cup of Gold*, of 1927 - was not a success, not least because the United States, like the rest of the world, was about to slip into the terrible economic crisis that affected the lives of millions of people for several years. In a short time, the banking system collapsed under the weight of the withdrawal of capital by panic-stricken customers, unemployment hit 12-15 million people in the US alone, about a quarter of all workers in the entire country. At least 60 per cent of households could not even scrape together $2,000 a year, a barely survivable figure, farmers saw the price of their produce plummet, and found themselves with an income reduced by two-thirds of the normal amount.

During the crisis, the first to jump are naturally luxury products and books in a certain sense are, because reading is considered something superfluous. So, Steinbeck wrote and sent manuscripts to various publishing houses, with no results other than to have them sent back. But, despite everything, he was not doing too badly. In 1930, he had married Carol Henning. He had a cottage in Pacific

Grove - right on the ocean - and a small income that his father passed on to him. John himself writes about that period:

> The depression did not affect me financially. I had no money to lose, but, like millions of people, hunger and cold did not appeal to me. I had two resources. My father owned a tiny three-room cottage in Pacific Grove, California, and he let me live there for free. First security. Pacific Grove is by the sea. Second security. Those who lived inland or in the stifling enclosure of industrial cemeteries had worse problems. With the sea on the side, you really had to be stupid to starve to death. This large reserve of food is always available [...]. Wood for the stove could be found every day on the beach, all it took was a saw and an axe. The cottage had a garden of black earth [...][2]

These few lines have an almost amused tone and perhaps Steinbeck really did regard those green years of his as a serene period. From the point of view of writing, he had continual disappointments, not only with *The Cup of Gold*, but also with *To a God Unknown* (1930) and *The Pastures of Heaven* (1931), which did not bring the hoped-for gains. From this period, however, is his meeting with Edward Ricketts, the person who, of all those close to Steinbeck, influenced his thought and work in a decisive way. He was a well-known figure in the area, owner of a marine analysis laboratory, part doctor, part sage, part philanthropist, part philosopher. Their friendship remained strong for almost twenty years, until Ed died in his car when he was run over by a speeding train. Ed also appears in various guises in several of Steinbeck's later novels, explicitly in the character of 'Doc' in *Cannery Row* and *Sweet Thursday*, but he is also overshadowed in such figures as Doctor Burton in *In Dubious Battle*, in Casy in *The Grapes of Wrath* and in Doctor Winter in *The Moon is Down*. With him he later made a long voyage across the Gulf of California that led to *The Log from the Sea of Cortez*.[3]

In the mid-1930s, things were about to change dramatically for John. He had just published the comic novel *Tortilla Flat* (1935), which recounts the wacky exploits of Danny and his wandering band of friends, all *paisanos* from Monterey, the last descendants

---

2   Steinbeck, *L'America e...*, cit., p. 41.
3   W. French, *Steinbeck*, la Nuova Italia, Florence 1969, p. 7.

of Californians with Spanish blood. The novel was written in a short time, at a terribly difficult time in John's personal life, his mother suffering a stroke and his father on the road to physical and mental decline. They both died shortly afterwards, within a year of each other. Yet the comic book, which came out quietly, was an unexpected success, even bringing Steinbeck, in addition to his first notoriety, the sum of 4000 dollars paid by Paramount to make a film of it. Things had changed and John's life was about to enter a new phase. This was also the moment of his meeting with Pascal Covici - who would remain his editor for life - and Elizabeth Otis, who, in partnership with Mavis MacIntosc, became his agent.

During the crisis years, we had witnessed the tremendous phenomenon of internal migration within the United States by entire families in search of chance of survival; squeezed into old Fords, these new nomads moved from the central part of the country to California, hoping to find work as labourers on coastal estates. Hordes of desperate people wandered around with the only asset being their truck or the car that contained all the family's possessions and was perhaps even their only hope of salvation. Steinbeck, to write some articles about these people,[4] came into contact with a world he did not know and was fascinated by it:

> In the first months of the migration, some groups were trapped by weather problems [...]. I had a friend, George West, from the San Francisco News, who asked me to go and write an article [...]. What I found was terrifying. We were just poor, but these people were really starving. Rejects in the mud, they were wet, hungry and desperate. And they were good, brave people. They won me over completely. I wrote six or seven articles and then did what I could to try to find them food. The locals were scared. They did what they could, but it was only natural that fear and, perhaps, pity, made them loathe that dirty, helpless swarm of locusts. The newspaper paid me, and since things were better for me at that time, I tried to live with them, even visited their places of origin to understand why they had left them. It was not philanthropy. I liked these people. I found their humour, courage, creativity and energy fascinating. I thought that if we had a national genius, it would be

---

4   The articles are collected in the book: J. Steinbeck, *I nomadi*, Il Saggiatore, Milan 2015.

these people, whom some were beginning to call 'Oakies', who would represent it[5]

It is from this experience that the novels *In Dubious Battle* (1936) - which recounts an attempt at a workers' strike, where the opposing cynicism of the owners and the organisers of the protest themselves, who exploit the desperation of these poor people for political ends - and above all *The Grapes of Wrath* were born. In Steinbeck's mind, the idea of writing 'the great book' had already taken shape after his encounter with the 'Oakies', because the narrative potential of this terrible affair of poverty appeared immense to him, as it could effectively highlight a true national drama, but also the condition of a wounded humanity. The attitudes, situations, and behaviour of the emigrants he had come to know so closely easily entered the flow of his creative activity, giving rise - between May and September 1938 - to a novel of 200,000 words, complex and very varied in tone and style.[6] *The Grapes of Wrath* was published in April 1939. It triggered immediate controversy from the Farmers' Association and a large section of public opinion, which branded it as 'communist'. However, it sold over 200,000 copies in a few weeks, the film and graphic rights were acquired for $75,000, one of the highest sums ever paid up to that time, and soon came the National Book Award and, above all, the Pulitzer Prize. The fame and controversy in which the writer found himself enveloped threw him into a severe depressive crisis, making him paranoid, suspicious, and distrustful, more so than he already was by character. It was a difficult period, from which he emerged mainly due to his meeting with Gwyndolyn Conger, to whom he married after divorcing his first wife. He moved with her to New York, a city from which he had already been rejected several years earlier in a previous attempt to fit in in his youth.

That time, he had supported himself with the help of his sister, with a job as a labourer during the construction of Madison Square Garden (not the current one, built in the 1960s, but the previous one, which opened in 1925) and failing a few attempts at journalistic collaboration, before returning almost desperately to California.

---

5   Steinbeck, *America and...*, cit., p. 47.
6   F. Garnero, *Come leggere John Steinbeck*, Mursia, Milan 1990, p. 43.

This time, the premises were completely different. Steinbeck was a personality, he was rich, he was a successful writer, even though he was always looked down upon by the New York intelligentsia, as if he continued to have on his jacket the country boy's dust and dirt on his hands.

Meanwhile, the Second World War was raging. John became involved in a project launched by President Roosevelt to combat Nazi propaganda with films and radio broadcasts. He worked as a consultant in these activities, as well as writing *The Moon is Down* (1942), a novel inspired by an episode in the Norwegian resistance, the message of which was mainly entrusted to Mayor Orden's words to the leader of the invaders, shortly before he was shot:

> Peoples do not like to be conquered and therefore will not be conquered. Free men cannot start a war, but once it has been started, they can continue to fight in defeat. Herd-men, followers of a leader, cannot do this, and that is why it is always herd-men who win battles and free men who win wars [...].[7]

For Steinbeck, war was merely a reaction of the unconscious, something irrational, he did not feel drawn to it, he had no desire to prove his manhood in combat. He did, however, commit himself out of a sense of loyalty to the nation. He even prepared a commissioned book on the American Air Force (*Bombs Away*, published in 1942) and also went to the front as a correspondent, confronting himself with the life of the soldiers. He wrote an entertaining book for them, *Cannery Row* (1942), where Ed Ricketts' philosophy of existence can be found: life and death count for nothing, they are only part of a process. What really matters is love and beauty.[8]

However, the influence of the marine biologist's thinking on Steinbeck's goes far beyond this somewhat simplistic perspective, almost the end of a long night-time conversation over a bottle of whisky. It is in- fact especially in the book that grew out of their trip together to the Gulf of California - *The Log from the Sea of Cortez* in 1941 - that this relationship emerges. From the pages of this volume,

---

7   J. Steinbeck, *La luna è tramontata*, Mondadori, Milan 2004, p. 180.
8   Garnero, *Come leggere...*, cit., p. 53.

important elements can be gathered to identify a system of constant ideas within the writer's oeuvre, despite the great variety of narrative techniques and topics addressed in the vast mass of his work.

There are three recurring models throughout Steinbeck's work. The first holds that man is a religious creature, which is why everyone tends to create his own divinity to satisfy his own primal need. The second, on the other hand, considers mankind as something to be considered from a biological point of view, a kind of group-animal, composed of individuals, but endowed with its own intelligence and will, distinct from those of the individuals that compose it. Outside the group-animal, there is another type of individual who observes and studies its behaviour. This can be seen very well in some of the characters in Steinbeck's novels. They are figures who somehow always remain outside the group-animal, able, because of their detachment, to observe others as if they were an object of study and they were biologists. They too are aware that they cannot have absolute objectivity, they are still part of that same humanity that they grasp at a distance, but they are at that moment detached from it and can afford the luxury of a different gaze. It is for this reason that such 'heroes' are admired, but also feared and misunderstood by the group, because, after all, they are outsiders. Such figures are Doc Burton of *In Dubious Battle*, Jim Casey of *The Grapes of Wrath*, Lee of *East of Eden*, Doc of *Cannery Row*.

The third recurring element in Steinbeck's work is 'non-teleological thinking', as the mystery whereby man lives without knowing the cause of his existence and, precisely this secret, drives him to seek moral values.[9] According to the writer, there are no deep links between cause and effect beyond physics. That is why there is no point in asking questions about the other meaning of things. This way of proceeding, 'teleological thinking', is in fact misleading, because it is only an attempt to change the conditions of a reality that is deemed unacceptable and ends up making the true observation of things impossible, and thus their rational understanding, the only one that can at least give man the possibility of acting concretely to change the situation for the better, if possible. It is necessary to

---

9   Ibid, p. 197 and pp. 204-205.

continue searching for the 'what' and the 'how', but to stop deluding oneself into believing that there is a 'why'. It is like moving through a labyrinth. Teleological thinking leads to dead ends, to illusions of an answer and thus stops the search, while non-teleological thinking strives to understand the whole complex situation, trying to lay the foundations for intelligent action. This is preferable according to Steinbeck to the false security born of illusion.[10]

It was not easy for John to hear the news of his friend Ed's death. It was also a time of rethinking, of radical changes. He had two children, but in 1949 he divorced their mother and, in 1950, married for the third time to Elaine Scott, a Texan and the daughter of an oilman. These were years of long trips to Europe and Russia, of much socialising, of magazines and journalists, but also the years for a necessary search for new themes for his work as a writer. For an author who had always based his stories on the concrete, on a precise context, on real people, on familiar places, it was now a question of finding new ideas in a life that was almost like a wanderer, far from the land that had most fertilised his inspiration and, above all, in a different and now rarefied world climate. His farewell book from his California had been *East of Eden* (1952), the story of a family through several decades, a tale brought to the screen by Elia Kazan, starring James Dean, in 1955.

This was followed by some radical attempts at renewal, some unsuccessful, such as the fanciful novel *The Short Reign of Pippin IV: A Fabrication* (1957), in which Steinbeck imagined France once again having a monarch, and others decidedly more interesting. In 1960, he set off with his dog across the booming United States in search of contact with the country's ordinary life. The result was the account of that adventure, *Travels with Charley: In Search of America* (1961), on the other hand, constitutes the testimony of an effort to establish a relationship with a community other than the Californian one of reference. The story is set on Long Island, where Ethan Hawley, a descendant of an old whaling family, is reduced to working as a clerk in a shop he once owned. He is an honest, responsible man with a great sense of guilt towards his family. It is

---

10   Ibid, pp. 208-209.

precisely this that spurs him to plot a series of cheats and betrayals that will bring him the much sought-after riches, but will also lead him to a bleak crisis of conscience.

For Steinbeck, meanwhile, the moment of consecration had arrived. In 1962, coming out of the bedroom in his pyjamas, he switched on the television to be informed about international political matters. Instead, he heard his name being announced as the winner of the Nobel Prize for Literature. During the press conference, he declared that he did not consider himself worthy of the prestigious award.

However, his life was coming to an end. These were the years of the Vietnam War, an extremely hot topic in the United States that became the main theme of his last writings. His positions fluctuated, from an initial one of doubt about American intervention, he moved on to strong support for the country's policy, only to later return to reservations about armed engagement. The roots of his views on what was happening in the Far East lay in his first-hand knowledge of Russian communism. The totalitarianism of the Soviet state, with its complete lack of freedom of thought, absolute control and conformism brought about by constant fear constituted for Steinbeck man's worst enemy, the horror realised on earth. That is why, from his point of view, the attempt by the USSR and China to extend this hell was to be fought by all means. And once again, he wanted to go in person to see the places, the troops engaged on the front, he wrote about it and talked about it, as he knew how, perhaps without really being able to take a sufficiently objective view of the matter. However, he was ill with heart disease, he suffered from emphysema, his arteries were clogged. 1968 was a year of fatigue, in which the energy of the massive Californian slowly ran out, until his death on 20 December of that year.

6
AN INTEGRATED MOVE:
JOHN FANTE

6.1 *Forgetting Bandini*

In the seventies, after a life lived on the fringes of society, Charles Bukowski had arrived at success; his books were read, translated, sold by the thousands, his ideals embraced by the beat generation and his name passed from mouth to mouth like smoke among the youth of the time. At the same time, an author to whom he owed a great deal from a literary point of view had fallen completely into oblivion: John Fante. His pen had produced some of the books to which dozens of writers who had come to Los Angeles in search of success had clung, lives often ruined, lives spent floundering, lives sometimes saved by the arrival of an unexpected success. Lives that retraced the epic described in Fante's most famous book, *Ask the Dust*, which tells the story of the impossible love between the ambitious writer Arturo Bandini and the beautiful Mexican waitress Camilla, in the context of a Los Angeles watched from the sidelines, populated by loneliness incapable of redeeming itself.

Bandini, therefore, like the young Bukowski: unknown, unhoped-for, taken on as an alter ego by the poet in search of a way, a companion of the same destiny. That is why Bukowski could not forget him when he reached the height of success. In his 1978 novel *Women*, this short dialogue appeared:

'Shoot'.
"Who was your favourite author?" 'Jack'
"Who?"
"John F--a--n--te. *Ask the Dust. Wait Until Spring, Bandini*". "Where are your books?"

"I found them at the City Library, downtown. Fifth and Olive, right?"
"Why did she like it?"
'Total emotions. A very brave man' .[1]

This simple homage by an acclaimed author constituted for John Fante the beginning of an extraordinary rediscovery, the return to the limelight of a writer who had experienced an incredible creative season during the 1930s, achieving notoriety and strong critical recognition, before disappearing again along paths of a creative, but less literary life.

His story had begun in Denver on 8 April 1909, where he was born, the

> first of four children, to a decidedly ill-assorted couple: the bricklayer from Torricella Peligna (Abruzzo) Nicola Fante - Americanised as 'Nick'

- and Mary Concepta Capolungo, of Lucanian origin, but born in Chicago. How the two met and what the shy girl found in a character as cluttered as her future husband is unknown. What is certain is that for the rest of her life, she remained faithful to that family and that union, despite the myriad storms that always characterised their daily life. Nick, in fact, was an excellent bricklayer - when he was sober - while in his alcoholic moments, which were quite extensive over the day, he became violent, quarrelled with everyone outside and inside the house, pursued fatuous gallant adventures and lost the little money playing poker in a club in Boulder. He had moved to this town with his family after leaving Denver.

They lived at 959 Arapahoe Road, in a house without a bathroom, with a coal stove. On cold Colorado winter nights, the brothers slept together in the same bed. Next to their home was a drugstore, run by a good man called Roy Clapp. Since the Fante family was often in dire financial straits, he never refused credit to poor Mary, who not infrequently had to resort to his generosity to put something on her children's table. John later spoke of this situation in the short stories Snowman and Put on the Bill, depicting with his usual tone between

---

1   C. Bukowski, *Donne*, Guanda, Parma 1999, p. 208.

the dramatic and the smiling the difficult situation of the mother, forced to the humiliation of always g o i n g shopping without money. The father, for better or worse, then found a way to repay his creditors with small jobs, but he remained completely unconcerned. Against this background, family life was bound to be stormy and serenity indefinitely absent.[2]

Yet, it is precisely this seething matter that became the foundation of John Fante's oeuvre, the figure of the father an indispensable presence, the thread of almost all his pages. That cumbersome, quarrelsome, egotistical man was in fact an irreplaceable element of family cohesion, a force of nature capable of holding everyone together, despite the quarrels, the insults, the unemployment of his character. This was perhaps his most extraordinary aspect, that is, the awareness of not having to yield for any reason to the dispersion of his affections, the will made of desperation and blood not to allow the crucible of his love to split. This sentiment is indelibly imprinted in Fante's work.

The writer was perfectly aware that his entire narrative imagery drew from that primal cell constituted by the life of his family. The brawls, the little big miseries, the humiliations, the unemployment, being Italian- American, the father's drunkenness, his betrayals, the beatings, all became fundamental themes, transfigured, however, in a style with soft tones, despite everything. At the centre of that universe Fante placed himself, in the deformed alter ego of Arturo Bandini, the protagonist of several novels and a figure within which the author could reveal and conceal himself at the same time. Through this mirror, Fante was able to give a new interpretation of real events, detaching them from all the dross of a dreary and peculiar everyday life, to make them a valid and comprehensible model of humanity for anyone, even for a real American who had no idea what it meant to be a "wop" or for any European reader who had never immigrated to the United States. In Fante there was a determination to follow a literary work of elaborating this material of familiar experience, a work that was also a search for style and expression in tune with the innovations of the best American

---

2   S. Cooper, *Una vita piena. Biografia* di John Fante, Marcos y Marcos, Milan 2011, pp. 36-38.

literature of his time. In this, the writer clearly distanced himself from the literature of immigration. For him, the epic of uprooting and adaptation to the new environment could not be a sufficient reason to make literature. The writer's work could not be exhausted in the simplicity of this thematic choice, but had to lead to the creation of universal models. Here lies Fante's distance from his Italian-American contemporaries, and here lies the ambiguity of which he was often the victim: an author who was incomprehensible regardless of his being the son of immigrants, but irreducible to a model of genre literature.[3]

Her beginnings had been decidedly difficult. By the age of twenty she was already clear in John's vocation for writing and also the realisation that, if any roads could be found, it was certainly not by staying in Colorado. Therefore, making an adventurous journey with no money in his pocket, he had moved from Boul- der to Los Angeles. Here he lived by changing jobs: clerk in an ice factory, worker in a tinned fish factory, handyman for a professional firm, scullery boy in bars and restaurants. It had been a whirlwind of jobs lost and found, of much wandering through the streets of the city together with many other young people like him full of hope, or simply unemployed, or even immigrants in even more difficult situations than his own. America was living through the terrible years of the Depression, yet John did not give up. He wrote to his mother towards the end of 1932:

> Dear Mum,
> Your letter with the postal order gave me great pleasure. You cannot imagine how good it made me feel. [...] Every penny weights like a boulder. I spend my time writing until things take a turn for the better. It is the most appropriate thing I can do at the moment, because I am determined to make a living by writing, and in no other way. Every writer has to starve a bit before he is worth anything. He has to experience the hard things as much as the easy things, and right now I am getting the ugly end of this business of living. Don't worry about me. Somehow I always manage.[4]

---

3   F. Durante, *Uno dei "big boys"*, introductory essay to J. Fante, *Romanzi e racconti*, Mondadori, Milan 2003, pp. XI-XIII and p. XIX.

4   Letter by John Fante to his mother, 4 October 1932, in J. Fante, *Lettere 1942-1981*, edited by S. Cooney, Einaudi, Turin 2004, p. 14.

And indeed, John found a way to get by. It was enough to make do with little, living in sordid motels on Bunker Hill or staying with friends during the worst of times. The days, however, did not pass in futility. The labours, the worries, the past condensed on the pages, giving rise to stories, to book attempts, to the first completed works of a man who week after week grew as a writer. He completed his novel *The Road to Los Angeles*, but failed to find a publisher willing to publish it. Too harsh, perhaps, too raw. The work remained unpublished until 1985, but the important thing was to keep writing.

The beginning of the correspondence between Fante and H.L. Men- ken, influential literary critic, essayist, editor, and head of the prestigious magazine 'American Mercury', dates back to this period. The young John had contacted him concerning his book *Treatise on the Gods*, saying he was enthusiastic about it and had submitted some of his writings. To that initial approach, Menken had responded with courtesy and interest: 'I don't see why you shouldn't achieve success as an author. You write clearly and your experiences provide you with a lot of material,' he reassured her in a letter.[5]

For Fante, the critic assumed the role of a true guide. It was he who blessed the young author's beginnings in his magazine, got him his first earnings and even put him in touch with some publishers. When in 1932 the 'American Mercury' published *Chierichetto* - the first work that came out - his name stood out on the green cover of the magazine, at the top of the list of the month's contributors. The old Nick was extremely proud of this, and from then on, he got into the habit of carrying in his pocket the crumpled periodicals in which his son's stories appeared, the very ones that portrayed him as detestable, whorish, violent, a drunkard. For him this was just a detail. The important thing was that John was making his way as an author and by now the ice was broken.

---

5   Cooper, *Una vita piena...*, cit., p. 81.

6.2 *Life of Henry J. Molise*

In 1937, John Fante met Joyce Smart, a fair-eyed girl, a Stanford student. Hers, contrary to the writer's, was a respectable family, Anglo- Saxon, Protestant, American for generations and enjoying a certain economic well-being. There could have been dozens of nice guys in whose arms the young woman could have ended up, but she liked those of the penniless writer from Boulder. When Joyce's mother heard the news of her daughter's affair with this hopelessly 'Italian' looking, unemployed character from a family of poor emigrants, she shut herself off in a menacing detachment. John was naturally not the type to be swayed by such an attitude, he was what he was: take it or leave it! He ended up being thrown out. Joyce's mother had intercepted the hand-written copy of *The Road to Los Angeles* that Fante had given to his girlfriend to read. The book could not, of course, please Mrs Smart. Too strong colours, scabrous passages, obscenity, and vulgarity.

Despite her mother's veto, Joyce did not lose interest in her John. The two continued to date in secret. They had at their disposal a wonderful Plymouth coupe that the girl had received as a gift for her 21st birthday, an ideal car for long getaways to places where they could be themselves. During one of these trips John and Joyce crossed the border of the state, reaching Nevada and then Reno, where they married in secret in July 1937. It was better not to let this news reach Mrs Smart, who had repeatedly threatened her daughter with closure if she did not break off her relationship with that 'wop'. And neither of the newlyweds was willing to give up that little bit of wealth guaranteed by the Smart family's money.[6]

They settled in Los Angeles, arguing frequently, mainly over money matters. John continued to earn little and spend a lot, also somewhat prone to his father's vices, especially drinking. Between the two of them, however, there was passion and true love, so, following a stormy navigation made up of shipwrecks and stretches of pleasant moonlight rolling, they stayed together for life, even having four children. It was a fruitful time, despite everything.

---

6   Ibid, pp. 149-156.

In three years, between 1938 and 1940, Fante published three small masterpieces: *Wait for Spring, Bandini, Ask the Dust* and the collection of short stories *Dago red*. The first book, dedicated to his childhood in Boulder, is the one that inaugurates his biography mirrored in the character of Arturo Bandini. All the figures of his life, particularly those of his father and mother, can be found in the novel. Of the four books dedicated to Bandini, this is the most ethnic, the one where Fante best tries to clarify his situation as an Italo-American, also inserting the element of religion, of being a catholic in a Protestant world, trying to show what this means and striving to focus on the problems of his immigrant family. For this reason, much more frequent than in other Bandini is the use of Italian, an Italian punctuated by the typical errors of Italian-Americans.[7] We also find many echoes of this world in the collection *Dago red*, but less so in *Ask the Dust*, a novel where the question of the young writer in search of a way out takes shape. Here too, there is no lack of ethnicity, but it is expanded into a new, 'integrated' perspective. Arturo loves a Mexican girl without being reciprocated. The girl, in turn, is rejected and not understood by an American bartender, of low social standing, but wasp. As the son of immigrants, Bandini can well understand the drama of the young woman, yet he is on a different level, because he was born in the United States and does not wear the marks of his ethnic diversity on his face.

These books were well received by the critics, much less so by the sale. A state of financial precariousness therefore persisted for Fante. In Los Angeles, however, the fatuous lights of Hollywood had been shining for some time. Big-money producers were looking for writers and authors to co-opt into the promising film production industry. The sums of money they could offer for a screenplay were not even close to those made available by a publisher. An up-and-coming writer like Fante could earn a maximum of 50, 100 dollars in a month for working on a book, while being employed by a producer the salary was 250 dollars a week. How to resist these sirens?

---

7   Durante, *Uno dei 'big boys'...*, cit., pp. XX-XXI.

Dear Mum,
[...] this morning I went to the Mgm film studios in Culver City. There I met some bigwigs in the script department who were very nice to me and made me a good offer for a story. [...] The amount of money they pay for stories took my breath away. For a good script they will give me five hundred to two thousand dollars. I have a really good opportunity. Tomorrow I will work on an idea, and by next week it will be finished. If Mgm likes the script and they buy it, the person who wrote it gets a three-month contract [...].[8]

John therefore swam to the island of Hollywood sirens. The choice paid off in terms of financial well-being. His wallet swelled very quickly, the days of cold nights in Boulder, of the grocer where he could buy on credit, of Bunker Hill motels disappeared. From flat to flat, as the family grew, Fante arrived at the splendid Malibu mansion, with swimming pool and ocean view, at Point Dume:

Our house was on an acre of land a hundred metres from the cliff and the roaring ocean below. It was an ipsilon-shaped rancho surrounded by a concrete wall that completely enclosed the land. A hundred and fifty tall pine trees grew along the wall, it was almost like living in a forest, and the whole thing looked like what it was not - the residence of a successful writer.[9]

The money had indeed arrived, but the work for Hollywood had taken up most of Fante's creative energies. Between the Thirties and the Sixties, John wrote hundreds of scripts and film subjects, but only a dozen of them actually served to make the films. Producers were fickle, many projects were ordered and then abandoned to direct the authors towards new themes. It was work done and thrown away, dropped, and picked up again and again. As any writer lent to the world of cinema experiences first-hand, John also realised that the scriptwriter's and the novelist's professions are not reconcilable. One engulfs the other. In fact, the creative process is completely different, the use made of writing has opposite purposes, the rules of the game

---

8   Letter by John Fante to his mother, 4 January 1933, in Fante, *Lettere...*, cit., p. 22.
9   J. Fante, *Il mio cane stupido*, in Fante, *Romanzi e racconti...*, cit., p. 969.

change radically. When you make a screenplay, you aim to provide a common tool for dozens of people with different professional skills - directors, actors, costume designers, set designers, musicians, find stuff... the text is just a plot, made to be changed countless times by the various figures involved in the production process, right up to the start of shooting. The story is only sketched out, defined by a series of small, concatenated splinters. The novel, on the other hand, lives solely on the writing. It is the one that shows the way, provides the climate, allows one to delve calmly into the world being told. It requires energy and solitary work. This is what the fiction writer desires, this is the work to which he feels called. That is why scriptwriting is for a storyteller fatally frustrating. Fante despised it: 'Writing for the cinema is a completely different thing from writing books. It takes no brains to put a film together. Any idiot can do it, and there is a tremendous amount of idiots in this town who get rich producing crap for the cinema'.[10]

There were few novels and short stories he could produce during this period and slowly slipped to the margins of the American literary scene. The price John paid for financial well-being was quite high in emotional terms and in terms of his writing career, but it was all in all a good compromise, much better than those most writers have to accept today. Fante still managed to produce some weighty novels.

Full of life is from 1952 and recounts in a decidedly mellow way his cohabitation with Joyce and the birth of their first child. It was supposed to be a fifth stage in Arturo Bandini's journey, but its tone was too soothing. Fante had not been Bandini for so long, he had Hollywood money, he had respectability, he no longer felt the anxiety of struggle, the polemical spirit. That is why the publisher convinced him to use real names for the characters, including his own. The novel marks in this sense a transition point. John was now ready to abandon his first alter ego and give birth to a new literary self, a more mature, gentrified and even moneyed writer. He was Henry J. Molise, the one who would be the protagonist of the novels *My Dog Stupid* and *The Brotherhood of the Grape*.

---

10   John Fante's letter to his mother, 12 July 1934, in Fante, *Lettere...*, cit., p. 77.

In these books too, the element of the family remains fundamental, and is explored along two distinct lines. In *My Dog Stupid*, perhaps Fante's most extravagant work, born in a period of generational confusion and revolution - from hippies, to the Vietnam War, to the psychedelic subculture -, John finally overcomes the position of the eternal adolescent embodied by Bandini to finally become a family man, pre-occupied with keeping his effervescent family unit together, with children on the run and lost in the difficult transition between youth and adulthood. In this Henry Molise ends up proving to be much more like the old Nick than he ever wanted to be.[11] And perhaps for this recognition, he dedicates one of his most touching novels to him, *The Brotherhood of the Grape*, in which the figure of the father is crystallised in an unforgettable portrait.

The time was finally ripe for Bukowski's rediscovery, but at that time John Fante was unfortunately already destroyed by the serious consequences of diabetes that had undermined his health. By now blind, he dictated *Dreams from Bunker Hill* to his wife, reviving that Arturo Bandini in whom his story of a man in search of a way was embodied and with whom many other writers had identified and continued to identify.

---

11   Durante, *Uno dei 'big boys'...*, cit., pp. XXV.

PART II
THE SUFFERED SPLENDOUR OF LIVING
O'Connor, Salinger, Kerouac, Carver

1
THE UNITED STATES
OF THE 1950S AND 1960S

The life of the average American at the beginning of the 1950s was supposed to be the one depicted in the many advertisements for the new electrical appliances: modern, bright kitchens, smiling women opening large ovens with steaming roasts, gardens watered and tended by mowers, cottages lined up in the new suburban districts, two cars in the garage, chubby children - preferably blond ones - in front of a beautiful television set. This glossy magazine *American Dream* existence appeared, in the common mindset, to be solidly guaranteed by an unsinkable economy and a benevolent state, the mirror of a country recognised throughout the world as the champion of goodness and democracy.

If this was the fake world where millions of people really lived - or tried to live - the reality was very different, even more troubled than it had been under the glitter of the 1920s.

The Second World War for the United States had been much more intense and shocking than the first. Their territory had been touched and the army had been massively involved, suffering numerous losses. After the conflict, the country found itself no longer just a planetary power, but even a hegemonic one, sharing its position with the Soviet Union. The tension with the former allies had escalated into the 'cold war' and the clash of the two blocs. Whilst the Stalinist USSR, encouraged by the Yalta Accords, had annexed the Eastern European countries into its sphere of influence, the United States had proceeded with a rapid Americanisation of the Western states, mainly through the reconstruction aid known as the Marshall Plan, and the creation of NATO, which allowed the new allies, including the Germans, to be rearmed. Against this backdrop, the chilling threat of nuclear war hovered.

On the domestic front, such a prospect invited a return to isolation, as well as fostering a hardening of the social climate. Once again, fear gave rise to realities such as the infamous Committee for Anti-American Activities, which returned to target emigrants and trade unionists, or to make mandatory 'loyalty oath' for public employees. Soon the committee became an instrument of power of Senator Joseph McCarthy, who established a climate of suspicion and gave free rein to vendettas, unjustified dismissals, restrictions on emigration, and various highly undemocratic measures, also favoured by the climate of growing international tension. In China, Mao had in fact imposed his regime after the triumphant 'long march' (1949), in French Indochina and British Malaya guerrilla warfare began and in Korea a real war broke out. The country had been artificially divided into two zones on the 38th floor, in the north under Soviet control and in the south under US control. By the time the foreign powers withdrew, the North had invaded the South, prompting the armed intervention of the United States.

In this climate, conservative positions prevailed in the American presidential elections, well embodied by General Dwight Eisenhower, who lacked political experience but was much loved as a World War II hero. Despite the premise, the new president succeeded in ending the dangerous Korean War. Shortly afterwards, Congress finally struck down McCarthy's actions with heavy censure and the Supreme Court declared racial segregation in the school system unconstitutional. On the trade union level, too, something moved in favour of African-Americans, thanks to the revision of some completely unfair regulations.

Beneath the apparent calm of 1950s US society something was therefore changing. Women with golden turkeys were perhaps not all content to stay inside kitchens full of appliances and blond children thought it better to do other things than watch television on the living room carpet. Many reached university campuses, opened up to less provincial perspectives, as the first satellites began to circle the earth. A radical breakthrough was imminent. Over the horizon, Kennedy's new America was appearing.

At the time, the country had about 170 million inhabitants, of which at least 5 million were unemployed, mainly due to automation.

Externally, immediately after his election, the president experienced the embarrassing adventure of the failed anti-Castro landing at the Bay of Pigs (1961) and the subsequent Cuban missile crisis (1962), when, for the first time, the United States could be directly hit by Soviet atomic weapons. Kennedy's advent did not seem to fulfil the promises of the eve and his own dramatic end, with his death in the Dallas bombing in November 1963, soon put an end to his work. Yet, in the short period of his presidency, he was able to implement some important measures (such as the launch of a civil rights programme or the signing of the treaty against the proliferation of atomic weapons), but above all he was able to spread among the people that confidence and hope of a possible peace that allowed them to breathe a new air.

The country's real problems remained very serious, however, and society was riven by deep rifts. The black ghettos (Birmingham, Harlem, Chicago, Philadelphia, Rochester, Wats, Cleveland, Detroit, Newark, Washington) had been shaken by repeated violent riots, while the black masses were becoming politicised (Martin Luther King's Students' Nonviolent Coordinating Committee, Malcolm X's Organisation of Afro-American Unity, Black Panther Party). Anti-segregationist revendications were increasingly pressing and justified. After all, in the previous decade, only small sections of the black population had been able to benefit from the great economic boom, while most of the black community, who had also made an important contribution to prosperity, had seen their conditions worsen.

In this climate of tension, there were the sensational and never clear- cut political murders (John and Robert Kennedy, Martin Luther King, Malcolm X), the sanitised repression of the Black Panthers, the trials of white and black radicals, and student unrest. In addition, the proposal for an alternative society took shape, that of the hippies, the Woodstock concert, Zen mysticism, collective hysteria, and generalised protests. A broad movement of struggle against the Vietnam War was born, which was a powerful catalyst of different souls and deeply marked the decade. Dominating the protest was the white, middle-class, student component, but the lack of strategy and perspective meant that, once the war was over, the wave died out in a short time.

This whole wave of protest and yearning for renewal stemmed from the generation that grew up in the opulence of the 1950s, a youth eager to assert its individuality in opposition to the world and values of its parents. It was above all music that provided these young people with important reference points. Rock 'n' roll - which fused black blues and rhythm 'n' blues with white country - became a powerful tool for shaping the new youth identity. This gave rise to collective myths, behavioural patterns, ways of dressing, talking, and rituals that were able to drag millions of young people beyond the flatness of the previous decade. The 1960s thus took the generation-breaking function of rock to the extreme and, together with other stimuli, made possible the development of what was called counterculture or underground culture. This explosion of the 1960s disrupted every aspect of American life and transformed it forever.

THE GIRL WHO LOVED PEACOCKS.
FLANNERY O'CONNOR

2.1 *Life in Devil's territory*

Have you ever observed a peacock? He walks with absolute pride, exhibiting an attitude of detachment from all things. Nothing around him is really worthy of him, not even his master. If you are in his way, he is not the one who has to change direction. You would like to ask him if he realises that he is just a chicken. He is not even good to eat, he is expensive, he makes a mess, he spoils flowers, he digs holes in the ground. Yet, there is something about that bird that compels silence. We all await his wheel almost with trepidation, but there is no way to make him do it if he does not want to. When he unfurls his feathers, however, we find ourselves before a small green universe, with a galaxy of suns surrounded by a halo. Is this enough to make it special? We do not know. But it cannot be denied that we are struck by its detachment from everything around it, as if it knows something that escapes us. In this, the peacock almost becomes a symbol of the complexity of reality, an invitation not to stop at appearances, but to look deeper, where the mystery lies. Perhaps because of this call, Flannery O'Connor was fascinated by peacocks. She owned around forty of them, as well as dozens of chickens, pheasants, turkeys, ducks, and quails. In the quiet of her farm in Andalusia, Milledgeville, after the few hours she could devote to writing in the morning, she would watch them. For her, they were a tangible sign of a God who acts between the folds of reality. And this is a determining element for writing.

Mary Flannery was born on 25 March 1925, in Savannah, Georgia, the only child of Edwin Francis O'Connor and Regina Cline. Hers was a life that would hardly lend itself to a good action film. The essentials of her biography can be summarised in a few lines. In 1945, he graduated from Georgia State College in English and social sciences. He received a scholarship to attend the Writer's Workshop at the University of Iowa and to work at the School of Writers of Paul Engle, who was also the teacher of many other important writers.

American writers, one need only mention Raymond Carver. Under the guidance of this teacher, Flannery composed her first short story, *The Geranium* (1946), which was published and paved the way for several competitions. Thanks to the first chapters of her novel *Wise Blood*, s h e won a grant to go to Yaddo, near New York, a well-known foundation that offers stays to young writers. Here, she stayed from 1947 to 1949 and met people who were important to her life, such as Elizabeth McKee, her future agent, and Robert and Sally Fitzgerald, to whom she was always bound by a great friendship. It is precisely after a stay with them that she has to return home to undergo a kidney operation. Following the operation, her life changes radically.

She was diagnosed with lupus erythematosus, a chronic autoimmune disease that could not be effectively combated at the time. It attacks the internal organs, the joints. Flannery survives following a series of transfusions and massive cortisone treatment. Her father had died a few years earlier for the same reason and the writer already knows the fate towards which she is heading. She moves with her mother to the farm in Andalusia in the early 1950s and hardly moves from there. She looks after her peacocks, paints, and studies, maintains important correspondence with various friends, tries to cure herself. These are the things she does in the afternoons, when her strength leaves her. In the mornings, however, she uses everything for writing.

Her genius is immediately apparent to all. She receives several awards, two honorary degrees, gives lectures, the cinema takes an interest in her work, she is compared to Henry James, Nathaniel Hawthorne, William Faulkner and, with the latter, has the honour of seeing all her work published by the Library of America. However, she is diagnosed with a tumour that is successfully operated on. Once again, the operation triggers lupus, which this time is fatal. Flannery dies at only 39 years of age, on 3 August 1964.

From a quantitative point of view, O'Connor's oeuvre is not colossal: the two novels *Wise Blood* (1952) and *The Violent Bear It Away* (1960), 21 short stories, a collection of essays – *Mystery and Manners: Occasional Prose* - and her epistolary.[1] From a qualitative point of view, on the other hand, his production is invaluable, evocative, original, and capable of standing out for the profoundness of reading reality that she manages to put forward. Her view of things constitutes a clear choice of field, which is why she creates a certain prejudice around her, which nevertheless clashes with some of the most convincing pages of American literature ever. According to Flannery O'Connor, the reality we live in - the 'devil's territory' - is to be considered not only in its sensible dimension, but also as a place where the 'Mystery', such as God, manifests itself. She writes to a friend:

> In saying that the moral foundation of Poetry is to accurately define the things of God, I guess I am not far off from Conrad when he said that his aim as an artist was to do as much justice to the visible universe as possible. For me, the visible universe is a reflection of the invisible one [...].[2]

According to Flannery, God acts and communicates himself to man in an interpenetration between the two worlds. It is not the material that becomes spiritual, but the spiritual that descends to the level of matter, becomes incarnate. We are of course at the heart of the Christian mystery, that of a God who becomes man, of the infinitely transcendent that somehow becomes concretely experienceable, can be encountered. This has a radical consequence in scripture, because one must bear in mind that in such a perspective human actions cannot but be conditioned by this presence. This does not mean that

---

1   For Flannery O'Connor's work in Italian, we recommend: *La saggezza nel sangue*, Garzanti, 2010; *Il cielo è dei violenti*, Einaudi, Turin 2008; *Tutti i racconti*, Bompiani, Milan 2009; *Nel territorio del diavolo*, Minimum fax, Rome 2003; *Sola a presidiare la fortezza. Lettere*, edited by O. Fatica, Einaudi, Turin 2001; *Il volto incompiuto. Saggi e lettere sul mestiere di scrivere*, edited by A. Spadaro, BUR - Rizzoli, Milan 2011.
2   Letter from F. O'Connor to 'A', in O'Connor, *Sola a presidiare...*, cit., pp. 50-51.

God imposes anything, but that He always interacts with human beings, even if most are unaware of this or deny it.

Naturally, with this perspective, the writer clashes with rationalistic, historical deterministic (from Hegel to Marx to the various historicisms) and psychological positions that teach us to read every event in an intramundane perspective, in which coherence can only be achieved in the horizontal dimension, as a mechanical or ethical consequentiality.[3] Well, according to Flannery, if you deny this depth of reality, you enclose yourself in an enclosure that effectively makes it impossible to understand the true reasons behind people's actions, and your own vision as an artist is irreparably impaired. O'Connor further writes:

> The Catholic writer, to the extent that he conforms to the Church's viewpoint, will feel life from the perspective of the central Christian mystery: namely that for it, in spite of all its horror, God deemed it worth dying for. This should widen, not narrow, the writer's field of vision. [...] When I have been told that because I am Catholic I cannot be an artist, I have had to reply disconsolately that precisely because I am Catholic I cannot allow myself to be less than an artist. The limitations that each writer imposes on his or her work will originate from the needs inherent in the material itself, and will generally be more rigorous than any limitation that religion can impose. The complexity of the problem, for the Catholic writer of fiction, will in part be the presence of grace as it manifests itself in nature, and the important thing for him is that his faith does not become separated from his dramatic sense and his vision of what is.[4]

That is why the presence of grace in the world is for Flannery a decisive feature of her work as a writer. It is indeed a matter of showing through her stories the action of God in the world, an action that is silent and almost invisible, but which can be identified and certainly highlighted through fiction. The writer must have 'vision', such as the ability to discern in every situation the

---

3   L. Doninelli, *Nessuno prestava attenzione al cielo*, in O'Connor, La saggezza...,
cit., p. 209.
4   O'Connor, *Nel territorio...*, cit., pp. 94-95.

different interpretative levels of reality, which for Flannery is to be read, according to the classical tradition of biblical interpretation, as bearing a literal meaning, a moral teaching and a reference to spiritual reality.[5]

The main characteristic of this reality is that it is still created. God's creation was not a single act, accomplished once and for all and concluded in time. On the contrary, it is a process still in being. For this reason, the world is unfinished, and this incompleteness is the mark of evil. This incompleteness, however, opens up a positive dynamic, the setting in motion of dormant forces that can lead to fullness. Pain, sickness

- like the one Flannery suffered from - good and bad, denied characters, ugly situations, everything becomes a resource for the creative and continuous action of a God who acts towards a fulfilment of creation. Man in this state of rebirth is completely free, he is immersed in the place of possibility, where he can channel his own action into that of God, thus becoming in turn his own creator and fulfiller. Flannery again writes:

> One of the tendencies of our age is to use the suffering of children to discredit the goodness of God, and once His goodness is discredited, to have closed the account with Him. [...] Busy removing human imperfection, they are also making progress on the raw material of goodness. [...] In this popular piety they gain in sensitivity and lose in vision. If they felt less, other epochs saw more, even if they saw with the blind, prophetic, insensitive eye of acceptance, of faith. A tenderness that has long since been detached from the person of Christ is shrouded in theory. When tenderness is separated from the source of tenderness, its logical consequence is terror. It ends in forced labour camps and the fumes of the gas chambers.[6]

The statement is peremptory and, as always for Flannery, devoid of embellishments. To be able to read evil, man's failings as signs of an im- perfection to be fulfilled, vision is required. Without it, a sense of the absurd prevails in the interpretation of the world, precluding

---

5   Ibid, p. 45. Cf. also: A. Spadaro, *La letteratura nel territorio del diavolo. La poetica di Flannery O'Connor*, in La Civiltà Cattolica, 2001, IV, pp. 36-45.
6   O'Connor, *Il volto...*, cit., pp. 99-100.

the possibility of a true feeling of the tragic. This prophetic eye is fundamental to both faith and narrative. In O'Connor's poetics, indeed, the two elements end up coinciding: 'For the writer of fiction, to believe in nothing is to see nothing',[7] she states in a letter. Not every believer can be a writer, but people of faith have the right eye to be one. If, however, the sensitive eye prevails, detached from vision, a vague feeling of tenderness, of compassion, emerges towards the real. This, detached from God, ends up on a horizontal prospective that becomes ideology. If the understanding of the meaning of evil and pain is lost, then this reality inherent in life is seen as something to be expelled at all costs. One yearns for a perfect world without pain and suffering. This, however, always corresponds to an idea of what is good for humanity, good for all. The attempt to realise these paradises on earth has led to the disasters of which history tells, the prison camps and gas chambers. Precisely because the world is unfinished, even the good is not always easy to decipher. Flannery O'Connor's fiction is a continuous search for these plots of the invisible stretched between the folds of the world and launched into an eschatological perspective.[8]

2.2 *Writing instruments*

From the old black-and-white pictures, Flannery often looks at us with a knowing smile, one of those that you show off when you have to take a photograph without feeling like it. We see her among her peacocks, on the farm's porch, sitting in a sitting room, standing with her crutches. Most of all her sharp gaze and an expression that has a certain severity about it, one of those you would expect from a teacher ready to catch you out. And, indeed, stern Flannery was indeed stern about books and writing. Just read some of her judgements on writers and would-be writers. This, however, is

---

7   Letter from F. O'Connor to Shirley Abbott, 17 March 1956, in O'Connor, *Sola a presidiare...*, cit., p. 60.

8   On the question of evil in Flannery O'Connor, cf. A. Spadaro, "Non sono scrittrice dell'impercettibile, io". *Il mistero di Flannery O'Connor*, in O'Connor, *Il volto...*, cit., pp. 30-35.

above all a virtue. What we need from a teacher is sincerity, a real look at our work, a look that can challenge it and make us evolve.

Flannery O'Connor has never been a lecturer in any school, yet she has taught writing to thousands of authors. She has given several lectures on her craft throughout her life, prepared with great seriousness and read at seminars or meetings, which have become milestones. The booklet that collects them, *Mystery and Manners*, was edited by Robert and Sally Fitzgerald after his death in 1969, and is still almost a cult object for writers. In just a few pages, Flannery succeeds in establishing the meridian points that writing must set, shows the way forward, and highlights the elements by which a text can have the right to call itself literature.

According to Flannery, writing works by accumulation of details, by recollecting of data to three hundred and sixty degrees and by filtering through a long decantation within ourselves. This is one of the reasons why we need to learn to observe things. In fact, our perception passes through the senses, therefore within the concreteness of reality. It is necessary to start from here to tell a story. When we meet a person, we do not immediately know what is going through his or her mind. We can tell by the expression on their face, their gestures, their words, all elements that we grasp through our senses, even if they refer to immaterial realities - moods, feelings, thoughts, ... -. We can therefore only access the deepest sphere of man through concreteness. Narrative must therefore be immersed in reality, and the latter is its only material. This is why it is necessary to avoid telling a story through a series of abstract concepts.

The result of this way of proceeding is doomed to sad failure. The reader will not believe the story if the writer merely reports it. He must make it touch, feel. You cannot give compassion with compassion, emotion with emotion; you have to arouse them through the description of the people and the event, as in life. We are not moved because someone tells us to be moved, but because we happen to see or hear something, which brings us to tears. Indeed, one must bear in mind that when writing fiction, one is talking '*with* characters and actions, not *about* characters and actions'.[9]

---

9   O'Connor, *Nel territorio...*, cit., p. 47.

This means that the writer must convey feelings, sorrows, joys, worries, arouse thoughts, memories, through the actions of the characters and their material representation, starting from reality. It must be this concreteness that accompanies the reader. For this to be possible, however, the author must first immerse himself in his story. The magic - and also the extreme difficulty of writing - lies in the fact that when literature is real, it enables experience. But for this to be possible, the author must first venture into the story he is telling.

It is not necessary to plan every aspect of the story, to study the characters, to think out the plan of the work. It is necessary to set out, to be guided by the writing itself. The story and the words the artist uses to tell it are one and the same; indeed, it is the story itself, the characters, the climate, the situation that shape the language and manner of narration. There is no meaning of the story separate from the story itself. A romance is a way of telling a truth that could only be told in that way. Of course, taking all this living magma conjured up by writing, channelling it into a meaningful channel and leading it back to a readable story requires a certain expertise and a good capacity for abstraction. What is needed is the *habitus* of writing, a way of approaching this activity that is deeply rooted in the person and is cultivated over time through experience.[10] Flannery's short stories and novels, moreover, have recurring elements that give structure to her stories and derive from her world view.

An important element of his style is the grotesque. Often in fact his characters and the environments in which they move have distinctive characteristics. Some figures resemble animals, others have bizarre behaviour or are difficult to understand at first sight. This has often misled certain sections of criticism, which tended to place O'Connor in the vein of southern writers in the United States, among quasi-genre authors, accustomed to using the elements of violence and the grotesque to give their stories certain typical hues. In Flannery's case, on the other hand, the grotesque is a necessary element to narrate the complexity of reality, that co-presence of

---

10   Ibid, pp. 66-67.

good and evil, that incompleteness at the basis of his worldview. The grotesque thus becomes a kind of bell alarm, a distortion that strikes the reader and prompts him to take a deeper look at things, to the point of revealing reality as it really is.[11]

This element enters Flannery O'Connor's stories almost immediately. Usually, in her stories, one is initially confronted with situations of normality. Apparently, there are no elements that foreshadow a change in the balance. The point of view is that of the protagonist, almost always armed with an unshakeable certainty, be it a world view, a political point of view, a religious or sociological conviction. In the light of this idea, he sets up his whole life and tries to pass it on to others, as is the case, for instance, with the character of Sheppard, a pivotal figure in *the* novel *The Violent Bear It Away*. In this situation, a completely unexpected, violent event occurs, a real shock. In the case of the book in question, Tarwater, whom Sheppard had educated according to his principles in the certainty of their infallibility, kills his retarded son to assert his own freedom. The trauma represents the intervention of Grace. This does not mean that it is God who does evil, because it depends on the free actions of men. However, the Mystery acts in those acts, unveiling itself, launching new perspectives. Faced with these events, the characters are called to a conversion:[12]

I cannot allow any of my characters, in a novel at least, to leave things unfinished. This undoubtedly stems from a Catholic upbringing and a Catholic sense of history: everything moves towards its true end or in the opposite direction; everything, in the final instance, is either saved or lost.[13]

If the character after the intervention of Grace still tries to save himself, if he still believes that he knows the truth and acts for good following only his own vision, he will end up destroying his life and losing himself forever. The final pages of Flannery's stories always

---

11   Cf. M.S. Falagiani, Flannery O'Connor. *"Un cuore al posto giusto"*, in O'Connor, *La schiena...*, cit., pp. 385-386 and M. Caramella, *Introduzione* a O'Connor, *Tutti i...*, cit., pp. XI-XII.

12   F. Castelli, *Redenzione e perdizione nell'opera di Flannery O'Connor*, in 'La Civiltà Cattolica', 1994, I, p. 437.

13   O'Connor, *Sola a presidiare...*, cit., p. 114.

perfectly describe one of these outcomes. The end of the narrative i s a bit like the end of the character's life, as if he is already in the metaphysical dimension following death. Everything crystallises, choices have been made, men can no longer act. Saved or damned.

3
SALINGER

3.1 *Finally in* The New Yorker. *Salinger's beginnins*

Like Hemingway, Fitzgerald, Carver and other great writers, Jerome Salinger also struggles with all his artistic energies to get himself published as much as possible by the literary magazines we have mentioned - starting with 'The New Yorker'. And it was precisely the prestigious weekly accepted in 1948, within six months, three of the nine short stories - which were to be published as a volume in '53: *A Perfect Day for Bananafish* in January, *Uncle Wiggily in Connecticut* three months later and in June *On the Eve of the War against the Eskimos*. More than ten years of frustrated efforts by one of the most convinced and ambitious young writers of the 20th century in the USA are thus rewarded.

In some respects, the unrequited love of Oona O'Neill (daughter of Eugene, Nobel laureate and author of *Strange Interlude*), which ends worse when she marries Charles Chaplin, lashes Salinger in his self-love as a young man in search of self-assertion, drawing comparisons with Fitzgerald's love for Zelda Sayre - even if with a different outcome.

From a social profile, however, young Jerome should struggle far less than the author of *Beautiful and Damned*. Coming from the side of Park Avenue, with a wealthy father and a mother who was a former actress involved in New York society, handsome as a Hollywood star and of sardonic and nonconformist intelligence, he creates problems with his character. Confined to a tough military academy at just 15 years of age, in the following years he tries to pursue a satisfying academic career; but he will never get there and will suffer for it - two other elements in common with Fitzgerald. The status of a professional storyteller, the transition from do-it-yourself writer (which he never really was) to full-fledged artist was offered to him by the 'New Yorker', a weekly magazine that the Biographer Lingerian Hamilton thus describes:

> He was confidential, punctilious, and loyal; he was also metropolitan, not acca- cording to certain aspects his values could be considered traditionalist. Salinger had kept his eyes on it for years, eyes that were often frustrated and resentful, but piqued, all things considered, by the conviction that one day that would be 'his place'. In 1948, the certainty that he had gained safe access to the upper echelons had encouraged him to get out of the swamp of glossy magazines.[1]

Although young (he was 29 years old in 1948), he knows very well the differences between a novel and a magazine. The 'published writer syndrome' hit him at the age of just 21, in 1940, when 'Story' published Salinger's first story ever. On hearing the news, the author became exultant and began to fantasise about how friends and detractors would react. But when the second story appeared in the University of Kansas City magazine in the same year, the first doubts appeared. The big magazines prove inaccessible, depress him, and give him anxiety about his future, so much so that he runs away from New York for a few weeks (he flees to Cape Cod and Canada).

Uncomfortable in polite society - he oscillates between picking fights and trying to look seductive, regularly drinking too much to gain courage-, disillusioned by interrupted academic studies and the final rejection of the beautiful and elegant Oona, Jerome also harbours doubts about his own abilities as a writer. Only with the successes in the major magazines, especially with the completely unexpected wave of sales, reviews and interviews that followed the appearance in 1951 of *The Catcher in the Rye*, does he manage to find his own dimension - but only for the 1950s.

The experience of the Second World War is rightly regarded by the best critics as central to Salinger's life and work. In life, because the fighting, the dead and the extreme uncertainty on the front line soon consumed the not exactly robust nerves of the soldier from Park Avenue. In the work, because there are many stories focused

---

1   I. Hamilton, *In cerca di Salinger*, Minimum Fax, Rome 2001, p. 139.

on the war experience, always with a single theme: the survivor dramatically oscillating between the hardships of the front line and the difficulties of reintegrating into civilian life. Tangible evidence of this is the absolute masterpiece of Salinger's work (not only in our opinion): the short story *For Esmé - With Love and Squalor*. Reading its pages, one understands the profound truth of the commentary sentences on the back cover of the Einaudi edition of the *Nine Tales*: only those who have experienced war and children are capable of accessing the truth. The language tends between a less extreme colloquial jargon than in *The Catcher in the Rye* and intense reflections, always managing to capture completely unprecedented aspects of the reality that surrounds us.

Critic and translator Simona Magherini points out:

> the role of children, who are often the protagonists of the stories or who, when they are not, seem to be the only people with whom the protagonist manages to have more or less normal relationships. Just think of the figures of Sybil in *A Perfect Day for Bananafish*, Phoebe in *The Catcher in the Rye* and Esmé in *For Esmé - with Love and Squalor*.[2]

Moreover, they represent a kind of counterbalance, sometimes momentarily 'therapeutic', for the Salingerian characters, who are regularly inept and shunned by an everyday life that shows itself as a kind of over-pretentious Parent. Faced with the hardships of ordinary living, the only escape routes are represented by the memory of the past and the authentic light-heartedness in the world of childhood.

Precisely in the years between the end of the 1940s and the 1950s, when America proudly threw itself into the industrial, social, and cultural path of recovery from the war and the conquest of supremacy in the western world, one of its young artists undertook to show the cracks in the system of the *American way of life*. Parents firm in their pseudo-values of half a century earlier, schools and universities and military academies that hardly distinguish themselves in hypocritically imposing the chrisms of the western way of life, the race for wealth and the profound dissatisfaction that comes with

---

2   S. Magherini, *Introduzione* in Jerome Salinger, Hapworth 16, 1924, Eldonejo, Milan 1997.

it, the pockets of inner squalor experienced in conformist America between Truman and Eisenhower, with the atomic and 'red' fears around the corner.

A watch that does not belong to the protagonist but was given to him by a nine-year-old girl of superior intelligence and sensitivity, sleep as an illusory escape, the search for a rationality capable of providing answers to the meaninglessness of living, feelings to fill the existential void: and here is the conclusion with the light shining on the protagonist of *For Esmé*:

> It was a long time before X was able to put the ticket away and decided to take Esme's father's watch out of the box. When he finally did, he saw that the glass had broken during the journey. He wondered if the watch was, other than that, intact, but lacked the courage to wind it and see if it worked. He remained like that, with the watch in his hand, for another very long interval. Then, all of a sudden, almost ecstatically, he felt sleepy.

Take a man who is truly sleepy, Esme, and rest assured that he always has at least a chance of becoming a man again, with all his f-a-c-u-l-t-i-e-s intact.[3]

3.2 *Individualism or conformism. For or against Holden*

If you really want to hear about it, the first thing you'll probably want to know is where I was born, and what my lousy childhood was like, and how my parents were occupied and all before they had me, and all that David Copper- field kind of crap, but I don't feel like going into it.

> If you really want to hear this story, you might first want to know where I was born and what my lousy childhood was like and what my parents and company were up to before I came along, and all that David Copperfield stuff, but I really don't feel like talking about it.[4]

---

3   J. Salinger, *Nove racconti*, Einaudi, Turin 1962, p. 136.
4   Respectively: J. Salinger, *The Catcher in the Rye*, Penguin Books, London & New York 1951, p. 5. J. Salinger, *Il giovane Holden*, Einaudi, Turin 1961, p.

It is one of the deservedly famous incipits of the second half of the twentieth century - considering the decline of dazzling beginnings as the decades and centuries go by - that at the same time marks a watershed as only great works can do. It bursts into American society, by now rocketing towards prosperity and world supremacy (as already mentioned), but at the same time locked in a narrow *Pilgrim Fathers* congregation moralism. Indeed, it is difficult to remove the veneer of double witch-hunting from the 1950s: political, thinking of Senator McCarthy and the Rosenberg trial, the anti-communist obsession fuelled by the war in Korea and, at the end of the decade, by the Cuban revolution, the persecution of Chaplin and so many artists forced to emigrate; cultural and customary witch hunts, from Guthrie and Seeger (equating folk singers = subversives) to the beat generation (Ginsberg's powerful poem *Howl* is from 1955).[5]

Salinger weaves a kind of inverted hymn of the teenagers' generation at the turning point between the 1940s and 1950s, denouncing in his own way parental and national puritanism, the adult lies to mock the children. And what is this manner? To mock the adult world in turn, adopting slang that is more invented than real, contagiously communicating hatred for the institutions of family, school, business, and the world of work. The Holden boy, it is clear from the outset (turns of phrase are certainly not the chosen register of the iconoclastic 32-year-old author), tells his parents and professors to go to hell (except for his favourite, who is also not his

---

3. It is true that a new Italian translation came out in 2014: but we are fond of the classic one by Adriana Motti, thanks to which we discovered the Salingerian world. Thinking about what Moretti writes about what he calls 'world works', we wonder if *Holden* could not also be included in them: '*Faust, Moby Dick*,(…) *Cantos, The Waste Land, The Man Without Qualities, One Hundred Years of Solitude*. These are not just any books. They are monuments. Sacred texts: which the modern West has long scrutinised, searching for its own secret. Yet literary history does not know what to do with them. It does not know how to classify them; and it does not put them in the same class anyway. It treats them as isolated phenomena: single cases, oddities, anomalies'. F. Moretti, *Opere mondo. Saggio sulla forma epica dal Faust a Cent'anni di solitudine*, Einaudi, Turin 1994, p. 3.

5 An intense as well as very rich picture of this period is drawn by: F. Pivano, *Beat Hippie Yippie. Il romanzo del pre-sessantotto americano*, Bompiani, Milan 1990.

favourite again), goes whoring, he loiters as much as he hates any school, sporting or emotional performance, as he loves to dawdle, jumping from bus to taxi to epic walks of miles and miles through a New York City perhaps never captured so lucidly as by this barely adolescent maverick. Romano Giachetti rightly points out how Tom Sawyer and Huckleberry Finn are little angels by comparison:

> Holden was not acceptable because he turned upside down what America, victorious after the war and its innate isolation (…) took for granted in 'heaven on earth' (...): family harmony. (…) young people waited their turn, happy to be protected (…) never a film or a book directed at them, never their voice taken as testimony to anything. (...) Into this honeyed postcard, which America believed in, plunged Holden Caulfield - and it was a disaster! Holden had no right to lie, mock his teachers, act naively blasé, drink (…) it was unacceptable that he should break everyone's heads with the bogus duck story; he was bogus: a daredevil before his time, a spoil-sport, a violent and eccentric without reason - that hunter's cap, that money thrown to the wind, his phoning at all hours of the night. This was the character that enchanted young people.[6]

Salinger, however, reacted to his resounding success by entrenching himself for the second half of his life in a rancorous and stubborn silence - broken, moreover, in the 1980s with the court case he launched against the courageous author of the excellent unauthorised biography, Ian Hamilton. Paradoxically, he draws one of the most effectively iconoclastic characters in contemporary literature and then abandon it to the millions of copies sold - in other words, to the society in which everything is for sale and the person who denounces it ends up making a lot of money on it. For Salinger, what can ever be the solution to the society/individual conflict? The return triumph of the individual, that is, of individualism. Precisely

---

6   R. Giachetti, *Il giovane Salinger*, Baldini & Castoldi, Milan 1998, pp. 70-71. Who knows what the then 19-year-old Canadian and soon-to-be world star of classical piano thought of him, eccentric to the point of suspecting mental disorders, isolationist and a maniac of long phone calls at night to friends halfway around the world. A splendid portrait is the volume edited by B. Monsaingeon, *Glenn Gould. No, non sono un eccentrico*, EDT/Music, Turin 1989.

in the most conformist decade of the American twentieth century (even more so than the 1920s, which were at least shaken by jazz and flappers, literature at the highest level and the social sensibility of intellectuals), one of the few who have the courage to break the shop window with the merchandise on display, as soon as the gesture is made, withdraws his hand and goes about his business, turning his back on everyone. Fortunately, however, the crusade against Holden fails miserably - despite accusations in many churches, court cases, denunciations, press campaigns, and teachers being fired *en masse*. The protagonist is accused of being a 'depraved' and 'lurid' teenager, thus a medium that can influence young people to be less attentive about the 'red danger'.

Salinger literally closed himself off from working on the novel for an entire year - summer 1949/summer 1950 - publishing only the short story *For Esmé - With Love and Squalor*. He moved alone into a house in Westport, Connecticut, where he lived in the company of a large black dog.

When the book is finished and accepted by t h e important Boston publishing house Little Brown, the author is as annoyed by the publicity launch as by the reviews. When the book is released in bookshops, he flees for a few weeks to England (to which he has not returned since the war) to keep away from the commercial exploitation of the book.

An article in the New York Herald Tribune reads:

> Shortly before *The Catcher in the Rye* came out, Jerome David Salinger not only asked the editors of his publishing house not to send him reviews of his novel, he even demanded that they promise him. "This will give you an idea of what kind of a guy he is." (...) He tended to get annoyed already about his photograph on the back cover of the book. Too big he had said.[7]

Are these the first symptoms of the flight from the world of a decade later? Yes and no: above all, we are not interested in delving into this theme, which is, moreover, trite and rehashed, rather to be entrusted to expert biographers such as Hamilton or the pair Shields

---

7   Hamilton, *In cerca di Salinger...*, cit., pp. 151-52.

and Salerno (authors of a splendid and impressive work on Salinger published in 2013).[8]

He fears triumph: as evidenced by his behaviour tending towards 'success neurosis', moreover anticipatory. As for the terms of this triumph, suffice it to say that *The Catcher in the Rye* reached 4th place in the 'Sunday Times' bestseller list and remained there for a good seven months. But it is above all in the long run that the extraordinary performance is measured (it is therefore better to speak of a long seller): in 1968 it was declared one of the 25 best-selling books since 1895, every year it still sells 250,000 copies worldwide, while as of 2014, some 14 million copies had been printed in English or translated into dozens of languages on five continents.

Dedication to his art is another element that contrasts with the hype of such figures, bringing him into line with a colleague as different (but not too different) as Philip Roth. The help that his passion for the oriental world - yoga, religions, meditation, literature, music - begins to provide him with turns out to be decisive and in years that are not suspicious of the later Indian fashion of the late 1960s/70s.

After the remarkable success of the *Nine Tales* that came out in '53 - a double success considering that it was a volume of short stories - and the aura that cloaked Salinger's name for many students at colleges and universities across America, he experienced an episode that marked him and pushed him definitively into reclusion in the middle of the New England woods.

In Cornish, Connecticut, where he has been living for the past few months - once he had left his native New York, which had tired him out with its crowds in the streets and the traffic that was beginning to congest it - he befriended large groups of young people, showing himself to be an excellent pedagogue. The portrait he draws of one of them offers us an unrecognisable Salinger compared to that of the next 50 years:

> He was always a lot of fun. (…) He had a fantastic sense of humour, very dry. We were happy when he came in and I think he had fun too. He was always entertaining the high school kids, buying us food and

---

8   D. Shields and S. Salerno, *Salinger. La guerra privata di uno scrittore*, Isbn edizioni, Milan 2014.

drink. He was very interested in basketball and football games, but especially basketball games. After the bar, we would all pile into his jeep and go up to his house. The house was always open up there. At any time, it didn't matter. He was always happy to see anyone. (…) He was very sincere. There was nothing fake about him.[9]

In the autumn of '53, two female students asked him for an interview for their high school paper, which Salinger willingly granted. In fact, the dialogue appears shortly afterwards in the Daily Eagle newspaper, which presents it as a fabulous scoop. The whole thing is, of course, without the knowledge of the interviewee. It closes like this, as abruptly as definitively, any relationship with the press on the part of an embittered and disappointed Salinger. Another story begins, one of isolation and withdrawal from the world, manias of persecution and total rejection of the role of writer. But it is known that in the following decades he produced at least a dozen novels and collections of short stories. Who knows if we will ever read them and if they will perhaps disappoint us.

---

9   Hamilton, *In cerca di Salinger...*, cit., pp. 181-82.

4
JOURNEY THROUGH DESOLATION.
JACK KEROUAC

4.1 *Jack's double life*

In a photo from the early 1950s, Allen Ginsberg, Lucien Carr and William Burroughs look at us earnestly from behind thick, round, plastic glasses. They are in a flat, among friends, but are wearing smart trousers, shirts and ties still fastened, although they are not wearing jackets. Their hair is cut short, in order. In another picture, Jack Kerouac can be seen in a suit, also wearing an impeccable tie, and even tucked into an elegant coat. The former look like university students who, after months of study and iron discipline, allow themselves the small indulgence of stopping for a drink with friends before rushing home to go to bed early and not mortgage the new day's work. Jack, on the other hand, gives the idea of being an entrepreneur ready to go to a business appointment where he will have to make a good impression, appear reliable, balanced. Nothing in these photographs hints that the people portrayed are actually the souls of the 'beat generation', the transgressors, the alcoholics, the drug experimenters, the destroyers of rules and conventions, the friends who exchange women and, at the same time, experience homo-erotic relationships, the voice of an American discomfort disguised under the colours of a new apparent prosperity.

Apart from Burroughs, who was born in 1914, all the others were born in the 1920s and became men after the Second World War. They are imbued with that society they want to destroy and, despite their firm resolve to live beyond those rules, those social conventions, traces of that past remain on them. The transition from that old, grey existence to a new, glittering one will never be accomplished. No ferry will take that generation to the other shore.

When they brought their demands to the world's attention, the air of renewal seemed to blow with great force. These artists became the expression of an unconscious but living protest among the great majority of America's youth, who were fed up with cinema and popcorn. The 'beats', the blissful ones, they thematised and experienced the anguished anguished unanswered questions, the insoluble questions, the conflicting claims of millions of other people and seemed to be able to interpret them, as well as to be able to escape the cages of that society, with their wandering and dissolute existence. And yet this possibility of rising above such a malaise, of living free, of following an extremely emotional way of life, which went from comedy to drama in a matter of moments, all based on constant movement and life impulses, appeared to be without a future from the outset, incapable of finding a theoretical formulation that would give it fulfilment and prevent it from becoming a replica of a pre-established model.

Once the momentum is over, the 'beat' ends up damned, among the shards of an existence exploded into a thousand fragments that cannot be reassembled. When his destiny is not tragic, as in the case of Jack Kerouac, his poetics fails in breaking out of the clichés of the group, does not make the transition towards a new synthesis,[1] exactly as in the old photographs in which those protagonists are portrayed, stuck in a world that does not belong to them and unable to fully reach the promised land.

Jean-Louis Lebris de Kerouac was born on 12 March 1922 in Lowell, Massachusetts, to a family originally from Quebec that had emigrated to the United States in the late 19th century. His father, Leo, was a robust printer with an unreliable temperament, capable of sudden fits of rage and addicted to whisky. This was a passion he passed on to his son, along with his hair and eye colour. He did not work with much impetus; this forced him to change jobs often, and consequently also his home, depending on the financial situation at the time, which was never prosperous.

---

1   A. Filippetti, *Jack Kerouac*, Il Castoro, Florence 1975, p. 37.

Her mother, Gabrielle Ange Lévesque, was a more reserved type. Orphaned of both parents at a young age, she had married early. She constituted Jack's most important family presence throughout his life, the only woman always present in his existence - despite three marriages - and ready to welcome him at any time, his safe haven after excesses and life on the road. She was very religious and brought up her son according to the teachings of the Catholic faith. With him, she chose to speak *Joual*, the dialect of the area of Quebec where they came from. This will be Jack's mother tongue, while English will be learnt later, at school.

The family also consisted of two other children, one of whom, Gerard, died at the age of nine of rheumatic fever, when Jack was four. The children were very close. The disappearance of his brother constituted a major trauma for the future writer, something in which an unjustified sense of guilt and a mythicization of his figure merged, through idealised reading, mainly due to his mother's stories. This presence acted throughout his life in Jack's imagination, until the writer attempted to give it order in the book *Visions of Gerard* (1963).

As a child, his great passions were writing and sports. Physical activity was pushed by his father, who saw it as something male, while writing was judged negatively, the stuff of sissies. Despite this, Jack composed a collection of short stories and two novels in his teens. It was not to writing, however, that the young man entrusted his social redemption, but to football.

His massive physique, speed and a certain power made Kerouac a decent player, someone who could have made a career. His father had initiated him into the sport as a young boy and tolerated his passion for writing because it was counterbalanced by his success in this area. Jack had by then decided to be a writer, but only the old parish priest supported him in this choice, while for everyone else, friends and family, he would have to focus solely on football. In fact, he did achieve some success. After graduating from high school, his sporting skills were noticed by the coaches of some university teams. Of these, Kerouac chose Columbia in New York.

He arrives in the Big Apple in a flat in Brooklyn, where he lives with relatives and attends a preparatory year at the Horace Mann Preparatory School in the Bronx. The accommodation is not the best, two hours away from the school by underground, but it allows him to get in touch with the effervescence of the city. His new classmates open him up to broader horizons, taking him to jazz clubs, such as the Apollo in Harlem or the Golden Gate. The sporting activity is satisfying and Jack writes about music as well as sport.

In 1940, he became a freshman at Columbia, but already in the second game, in a game clash, his tibia was broken. His career as a football player is now decided, although it will take some time to realise this. Following the injury, the writer has a lot of free time. He spends long hours immersed in reading authors who will be determined for him, such as Hemingway, Saroian, Céline, Wolfe. He also begins his nocturnal exploration of New York life. In these underground pilgrimages he meets Allen Ginsberg and William Burroughs, abandoning himself with them ever deeper into that stray, alcoholic and amphetaminic spiral that will become a determined element of its existence. Their meeting point is the West End Bar, near Columbia.

After a brief stint in the merchant navy, he met Frankie Edith Parker, who was to become his first wife.[2] Also entering her life is Lucien Carr, rich, seductive, charismatic, the catalyst of their group. The young man suffers the unwanted attentions of an older man and ends up killing him. Jack himself is implicated in the affair, having helped the murderer to hide the evidence. For this he ends up in prison, from where he only gets out thanks to the financial support of Edie's family.

The two young people get married while Jack is still in prison, but the relationship is already on the rocks. The group of their friends live in a flat where open couples, bisexuals, homosexuals, prostitutes, various drug, alcohol, and amphetamine addicts meet. There is no rule in the flat, except that of excess, of getting high, of living beyond convention. For Jack, a schizophrenic existence begins, divided between life in the metropolis, where he loses himself in these environments, and life at home with his family, in the small town. He often goes to his mother's, clean-cut, tidy, behaving impeccably, and remains so throughout his time with

---

2   E. Kerouac-Parker, *La mia vita con Jack*, Stampa alternativa, Rome 2008.

her, then returns to New York and resumes the merry-go-round of excesses.[3] In the metropolis, however, Jack manages to write with great commitment, trying to put his life experience down on paper. He works frantically, destroys everything that does not seem worthy enough for him, and only takes short breaks at the West End Bar. He almost always writes under the influence of Benzedrine, in long work sessions. He does not care to self-destruct. He is trying to accomplish an important work and is willing to sacrifice himself to make a mark in the history of literature, to give his country's culture a shot in the arm. The effort is made worse by his father's illness, which soon leads to his death. Jack moves away from the city to be as close to him as he can, but he does not stop working. In 1948, that great ideal effort results in Kerouac's first novel, published under the name John, *The Town and the City*.

The book tells the story of the Martin family and is set between Lowell and New York, between 1935 and the end of the Second World War. The protagonists are two brothers, Peter and Francis, who have parallel lives and reflect the schizophrenia of Jack's own life. The small microcosm evoked by the story succeeds in restoring the sense of loss of innocence of the generation that had lived through the war. The model followed by Kerouac is that of Wolfe's river writing, but the echoes of Saroyan are also remarkable. The outcome is not the best.[4] Indeed, the critics of the time are rather cold towards the work, generating a deep sense of frustration in Jack:

> I spent four years without the joys of normal juvenile life to make a serious contribution to American literature and the result is treated as a cheap first novel, which it certainly is not, notwithstanding my 'apparent' success. *The Town and the City*, while it has weaknesses here and there, is on the whole a serious work, not frivolous, and such should be the commentary distributed around by the vain reviewers who do the same thing, day in and day out, with countless novels of all kinds. I am so confused that I no longer care to finish the sentence. Apparently as far as the commuting, bourgeois reviewers are concerned, there is

---

3   M. Corona, *Cronologia*, in J. Kerouac, *Romanzi e racconti*, Mondadori, Milan 2001, p. CI.

4   C. Scarpino, C. Schiavini, S.M. Zangari, *Guida alla letteratura degli Stati Uniti*, Odoya, Bologna 2014, p. 211.

nothing 'significant' in the novel except a portrait of themselves. My Levinsky was received as a useless madman, and the same was true of Alexander Panos: my Job-like father was called a mediocre, 'a death-defying lamentation of a travelling salesman'. [...] There is something corrupt in America if such things happen.[5]

Jack still does not stop writing. He does it in the following years in an even more frenzied, crazier way, getting help from Benzedrine and other drugs, throwing his existence beyond the confines of New York, through the endless streets of the United States. Life on the road is really about to begin.

4.2 *The fatigue of existing*

On a New York evening, at the usual West End Bar, some friends introduce Jack to a young man from Denver, Neal Cassady. He is a twenty-something who says he was born on the road, in Salt Lake City, while his parents were driving through Utah. His is a life on the road, spent in squalid hotels, hitch-hiking or hitch-hiking on goods trains, with the occasional short break to scrape together a little money by working as a dishwasher or fruit picker, or simply by pilfering here and there.

When they meet, Jack is immediately fascinated. The two physically resemble each other, are complementary in character and feel the same drive towards existence. It does not take them long to throw themselves into life on the road that Kerouac will celebrate in his later novels. With Neal, he will cross America in all directions, from New York to San Francisco, from Mexico City to Washington, losing himself in brothels and smoky clubs where jazz or be-bop is played, travelling by makeshift means, but above all by car. Legend has it that Neal has stolen over five hundred of them and is able to drive for hours on end without apparent fatigue.

Soon Jack makes his friend the archetype of the American hero. For him, Cassady is not an unblemished champion, but a raw character, endowed, however, with a seemingly endless energy

---

5   J. Kerouac, *Un mondo battuto dal vento*, Mondadori, Milan 2006, p. 348.

that keeps his vital momentum alive. His lack of inhibitions, his seething enthusiasm, his permanent excitement, his torrential bursts of conversion, his tirelessness, his unquenchable eagerness for adventure - all this makes Neal almost the reincarnation of the ancient myth of the pioneer and allows Jack to project onto him the image of himself, of how he would like to be. Kerouac's childhood dream of becoming a hero, later revived in the hope of emerging as a football player, can now be revived in the figure of Neal.[6]

Jack aspires to tell his own story and his own world, but every time he tries to write about himself, he ends up talking about Cassady. He still cannot, as Hemingway could, make his own life the subject of his fiction. He needs an alter ego. The 'Lost Generation' had been able to denounce the anomalies of the world and unhinge them with its own force and violence; the 'Beat Generation', on the other hand, finds itself immersed in a society where the issues have now come to the surface and must rather be in- dagated with a more inward-looking quest. The new protagonists cannot therefore rely on their own strength to change things, as their predecessors had done. They are more fragile, they must flee, hide in other lives. Cassady thus becomes the protagonist of Jack's work, which he perpetuates in many novels. The most famous, of course, is *On the Road*.

Although legend has it that it was written in only three weeks, the book actually had a very long gestation, lasting years, to which was added the transcription of the famous scroll on over four hundred and fifty sheets and the subsequent reworking imposed by Viking Press. The story narrated is that of Sal Paradise (Kerouac's alter ego) and Dean Moriarty (Cassady) and their wanderings across the United States between 1948 and 1949. One is a man from the East, grappling with a novel to finish, a failed marriage, and the recent death of his father; the other comes from the West, burns with an incredible love of life, and has a juvenile record. Both are in search of a new beginning, postponed, however, at each departure, in the mad rush to find old friends scattered across the continent, animated by the same restlessness and the same desire for transgression. Dean embodies the emblem of freedom, to be pursued at all costs. In fact,

---

6   F. Pivano, *Album americano*, Frassinelli, Milan 1997, pp. 72-77.

he will not hesitate to abandon his sick friend in Mexico City to resume his search for adventures, mirroring his generation's need to live in the moment, even burning himself with extreme experiences, made of alcohol, drugs and speed, necessary to forget his own existence, which has been blighted by consumerism and the atomic nightmare. However, there is no way out, no place to take refuge. The only possibility is escape, which however often coincides with self-destruction.[7]

The prose adopted in the novel is rhythmic, syncopated. In Kerouac's intention it was meant to be an evolution of Joyce's stream of consciousness, but it is perhaps more akin to the much-loved black music. It is a writing that seeks energy, immediacy, the same freedom that Kerouac's novels speak of.

The book became the manifesto of the 'Beat Generation' and propelled the writer into the limelight of instant fame, making him the centre of national interest equal to that reserved for film stars or sports heroes. Kerouac is taken by storm by television and radio journalists, speakers, newspaper critics, even sociological scholars. In a few moments, the unknown writer became a phenomenon of custom.[8]

To make the most of its author's moment of fame, Viking Press printed seven previously unpublished novels over the next three years, fuelling the legend of a Kerouac capable of writing entire books on the spur of the moment, regardless of form and style. This moment of overwhelming fame, however, also marked the beginning of the writer's definitive decline. Increasingly imprisoned by his public image of himself and his success, he ends up taking more determined refuge in alcohol, while his new texts lose their incisiveness.

The willingness of publishers to publish whatever he wrote prompted Kerouac to retrieve works written even several years earlier, to rework them, to give them new forms. The matrix is always his autobiographical experience, which now becomes the main subject of his production. In fact, at this point, the writer tends

---

7   Scarpino, Schiavini, Zangari, *Guida alla letteratura...*, cit., p. 213.
8   F. Pivano, *La balena bianca e altri miti*, Il Saggiatore, Milan 1995, p. 425.

to read his entire oeuvre as a unicum, fragments of his existence recounted in as many novels, a story he called the 'Legend of Dolouz' (echoing perhaps the Joycian Dedalus). The saga consists of ten books that retrace broad stretches of the protagonist's life: childhood (*Visions of Gerard* and *The Doctor Sax*); adolescence (*Vanity of Dolouz* and *Maggie Cassidy*); the experience of the street (*Visions of Cody*); maturity and the search (*Tristessa, Desolation Angels, Book of Dreams*); collapse and perdition (*Big Sur* and *Satori in Paris*).[9]

Between the folds of 'Legend', other works find their way. *The Subterraneans* was written in three days under the influence of Benzedrine and was published in 1958. The setting is the sordid and squalid one of San Francisco's drug addicts. The backdrop is in fact Telegraph Hill. Here the bleak existences of outcasts and derelicts gather, and these are the 'subterraneans' of the title, the world already known in other Kerouac novels, made up of highs, sexual promiscuity, and exclusion. It is against this backdrop that the love story between Leo Percipied and Mardou Fox unfolds, ending with the protagonist's abandonment of that world of excess for a return to his mother's house. Once again, a fact from the writer's true history is overshadowed in the story, his relationship with a black girl - ten years before the Civil Right Act - and his tension towards returning home in search of a refuge at the home of his deepest affections. This yearning for a place where one can finally shelter oneself from the 'subterraneousness' of life also manifests itself in Kerouac in the form of religious research. After having completely detached himself from Catholicism, he in fact tries to follow the path of Buddhism, though giving it a rather personal interpretation. *The Wanderers of Dahrma* marks an important stage in this journey, constituting the writer's most organic effort to present his reflections on this doctrine, which had matured during the period he spent in San Francisco with Gary Snyder, a poet and scholar of oriental religions. A group of friends, once so far from self-destruction, seek the definition of inner peace and discover that this bliss comes from reflection, contact with unspoilt nature and art. This last aspect is emphasised by moments

---

9   Scarpino, Schiavini, Zangari, *Guida alla letteratura...*, cit., p. 214.

of poetry reading, in which each person takes turns in front of the others proposing his or her own compositions.

On the part of the roll remaining after writing *The Wanderers of Dahrma*, still under the influence of Benzedrine, Kerouac composed *Big Sur*, which tells of his physical and psychic collapse under the great pressure of fame. After the great journey of *On the Road*, the author is on the move again, returning once more to California, passing through San Francisco and Los Angeles, to reach the town of Big Sur, where Ferlinghetti has put a small cottage at his disposal. The isolated place, however, does not allow him to really get away from his fame or even his addiction to alcohol. It now seems that the old refuges - the escape on the road or the solitude of unspoilt nature - have lost their saving power. Jack's crisis is deepening.

Big Sur is the author's last significant work. It came out in 1962, only five years after *On the Road*. As many as fifteen titles were published in this short period of time, but out of these ones no more than six were written after 1956. Kerouac's artistic and intellectual crisis is evident. The writer is increasingly obnubilated by alcohol - he now drinks more than a litre of whisky a day - and his relationship with his mother becomes increasingly morbid, especially when she suffers a stroke. There is no escape from Jack's tragic parable. On 20 October 1969 his liver fails, and an internal haemorrhage kills him at only 47 years of age. The year before, Neal Cassady had also passed away, probably due to an overdose. The death had been consistent with Kerouac's narrative, taking both 'off the street' suddenly, with no possibility of appeal, as perhaps Jack himself would have done with two of his characters.

5
RAYMOND CARVER

5.1 *Writing is the art of discovery. On Carver's short stories*

Novel and reality. However much the binomial may annoy contemporary critics and may seem worn out, there is no escape. We may assume that reality is another, involving heaven and hell, gods, angels, the apocalypse, and galaxies: but we owe the modern notion of reality as elaborated by Western culture to the novel and the natural sciences.[1]

It is only an apparent paradox that today's concept of reality derives from the novel form - as well as from the natural sciences, as the literary critic Berardinelli (a fine collaborator of the legendary *Quaderni piacentini* and animator of *Diario* together with Piergiorgio Bellocchio) points out. As we can see, we are still on the terrain of the double (the paradigmatic *doppelgänger* of German and Austrian literature, with its intense psychoanalytic flavour), which Givone mentions in one of the notes to an earlier §. In fiction, understood as making novels, each element can refer to one or more other elements, depending on the fineness of the analysis, as well as on the kind of reading that is being carried out (literary, linguistic, historical, philosophical, psychoanalytic, and so on). The style may differ from author to author, but it always means one thing: writing with honesty, originality, extreme care. It has nothing to do with length or brevity, elegance or the absence of ornaments, background noise or spaces of absolute silence, youth or old age, erudite culture or street culture.

---

1   A. Berardinelli, *L'incontro con la realtà*, in F. Moretti (ed.), *Il romanzo. Volume secondo: Le forme*, Einaudi, Turin 2002, p. 341.

Mozart is rightly (and finally) analysed by critics from Baumgartner onwards as a 'false simplicity', putting an end once and for all to the silly vulgate of a graceful rococo, smiling and *gentillettes* (Deleuze would say). With a nice leap in time and cultural territory, one can think of another example of a simple fake in the work of Raymond Carver: in the sense of passing off his unadorned and concise writing, bare to the point of the inconceivable, as the product in front of which the fools on duty comment: 'but it takes nothing to write like that'. Extreme greatness of the pseudo-inventor of minimalism - when it is he himself who protests against such erroneous attribution of authorship. Moreover, a distinction must be made between the version imposed by his main editor (as recently discovered) and the original Carverian version.

As can be seen, at a first quick and (this one) simple deprived, we are already faced with three sources of ambiguity (certainly not intended by Carver), or, if you prefer, three levels of reading:

- the apparent bare simplicity of the style and stories told;
- distance from minimalism;

The British sociologist of culture and historian of ideas Raymond Williams printed in 1961 *Culture and Society 1780-1950*, soon to become a classic, one of the most significant texts analysing the relationship between the development of society and the role of culture. Here are some very valuable reflections for the discourse we are conducting in these pages:

> The history of the idea of culture is the record of our reactions, both intellectual and sentimental, to the changing conditions of our common life.
> - the similar distance between the writer's workshop and the publishing industry.

Regarding the commerciality and publishing strategies of the last decade of Carver's life, with the double contemporaneity of success - his and the minimalists' - we are helped by the analysis we find in a recent text on the history of American literature:

With the 1980s, the structures and dynamics of publishing became more and more evident, together with the role play of the figures who concretely managed the destinies of 'American literature'. With the East Coast taking the lion's share, it is a dance of lobbies, publishing and distribution policies that sanctions the predominance of the figure of the literary agent (no writer who aspires to success is without one), or that of the editor (who decides editorial lines, commissions novels, and perhaps intervenes directly on the texts of his own 'authors'). Nor is there any shortage of godfathers, perhaps the very professors of those creative writing courses (...) nor perhaps the heads of the literary columns of periodicals such as 'The New Yorker', 'Esquire' or 'Harper's', who lay down the law in directing the readers' taste and market trends.[2]

The author of *Cathedral* asserts the profound difference between sloppy, imitative pseudo-experimentalism, and true experimentation understood as re- search, innovation, a strenuous path. He quotes Pound, reminding us that those who experiment must 'make everything new'.

Linked to this reasoning is the light that can be thrown on objects, the simplest, everyday ones, to endow them with a seductiveness and absolute capacity for the most unexpected references:

> In a poem or a short story, one can describe things, common objects using common but precise language, and endow these objects - a chair, the curtains of a window, a fork, a stone, an earring - with immense, even astounding power. One can write a line of seemingly innocuous dialogue and have it send a shiver down the reader's spine - the origin of artistic pleasure according to Nabokov.[3]

Thus, a poetics of everyday objects and dialogues emerges. Everyday life represents one of the sources of apparent reassurance; in reality it is in itself endowed with a profound charge of ambiguity. One thinks of the use of things, situations, environments that are apparently completely normal in the context of suspenseful situations

---

2   G. Fink, M. Maffi, F. Minganti, B. Tarozzi, *Storia della letteratura*, Sansoni, Florence 2001, p. 546.

3   R. Carver, *Il mestiere di scrivere*, Einaudi, Turin 1997, p. 8.

in films by Hitchcock or De Palma or early Spielberg.[4] The lesson of the object, of the everyday, runs like a single (yet different) *fil rouge* through the experience of modernity: think of the intense richness of Morandi's still lives, the restlessness that emerges in Magritte, Duchamp's invention of the ready-made or the objects described in the silent black and white of Wenders' first season.

To create narratives (in Carver's case) you need words - which is all we have, as he says - and so they have to be the right ones. A very simple domestic situation - a telephone ringing while vacuuming along the carpets - makes the narrator think that there could be a whole story behind that situation, familiar to anyone.

And where does the tension come from according to the Oregonian writer? From the manner in which the words (always them) connect to form the action of the story, which express its visibility. Narrator V. Pritchett, quoted by Carver, defines the story as that which is glimpsed out of the mere corner of the eye. But beware: as is often the case, the marvellous is de- posed in the details. So:

> The task of the short story writer is to invest that something just glimpsed with everything in his power. (...) And all this is achieved through the use of clear and precise language, language used in such a way as to breathe life into details that illuminate the tale for the reader.[5]

So, for the author of *Desolation Angels* the writer shifts the reader's attention to the neglected, the repressed (Freud would say). Thanks to words, what is before our eyes changes into the uncanny (the father of psychoanalysis again), enveloping us in its own apparent forms. Anything can then happen: bewilderment, wonder, fear, joy. One thinks of the verse in the first act of *Macbeth* in which Shakespeare - albeit in a completely different context - still performs a linguistic operation of mutation of a common object into a source of death: 'show thyself as the fairest flower, but be the serpent concealed therein'. One thinks, to quote Carver, of the

---

4   On Hitchcock's cinema see of course A. Hitchcock, *Hitchcock secondo Hitchcock. Idee e confessioni del maestro del brivido*, Baldini &Castoldi, Milan 2000.

5   Carver, *Il mestiere...*, cit., p. 12.

story in which a birthday cake to be delivered to the family of the birthday boy dies in the meantime in an accident. Not for nothing is it included in Altman's wonderful 1993 film version of *America Today*.[6]

Writing becomes the discovery of a sub reality, without the need to go looking for it in places other than those of our ordinary living - the cornerstone of Carveri's poetics is thus: 'writing is an act of discovery'. To get a small glimpse of Carveri's writing workshop, one only has to read the forty or so pages of reflections on half a dozen collections and one poem - all paragraphs with the simple indication of *About*. As, for instance, when he talks about 'messing around with stories':

> I like to tinker with my stories. I prefer to tinker around with a story after writing it and then tinker with it again later, changing one thing here and one thing there, rather than writing it the first time. The initial draft seems to me to be the hard part to get through and then go ahead and have fun with the story. Revision for me is not an unwelcome obligation - on the contrary, it is something I enjoy doing.[7]

5.2 *From degree zero to full form. Carver's workshop*

Just how inseparable Raymond Carver's writing, themes, and life is shown by the extraordinary dedication with which he committed himself to writing stories from an early age, always believing in them. Consider that he comes from a family made up of a sawmill worker and a waitress who belong to the marginal proletariat America, which their artist son will describe so vividly. The same way of living, dressing, the inhabited houses, the simplicity and a certain roughness, the drinking habit (abandoned with great courage a few years after his death) are characteristic signs of that America, of that working class, of that province. And this way of life persists, despite his intellectual activities made up of short stories, essays, creative

---

6   It is the short story *Il bagno*, from the collection *Di cosa parliamo quando parliamo*
d'amore, Garzanti, Milan 1987, pp. 45-53.
7   Carver, *Il mestiere...*, cit., p. 57.

writing lectures (so much so that he is recognised as the undisputed master, not of minimalism but of many young people interested in changing, once again, the course of American literature). The young Carver becomes the first high school graduate in his family. At Chico State College he met John Gardner, at himself a master of numerous writers.

For Carver, meeting John Gardner meant coming into contact for the first time with the intellectual environment he had always longed for. Until that moment, his existential heritage still consisted of his own experience of living in houses without services and without hot water, of initiatory fishing in the rivers of the North-West, of the obligatory silences of the sawmills. In a word, the solitude of the working poor.[8]

After two years at Chico, he went on to California State University, on the Humboldt County campus. In the following years, he worked as a sawmill worker during the day and studied creative writing courses in the evenings and at night, until graduating in 1963. He then attends two different interrupted master's courses (one as a librarian, the other again in creative writing). He then goes over to the other side, to professorships in various universities, as he publishes his short stories and various essays in increasingly important journals, and as his fame and esteem grow. He no longer has to work as a labourer, caretaker, night watchman, hospital orderly. But the abandonment of the working poor life leaves him with a profound knowledge and a sense of solidarity with the people who have shared his painful journey for many years to make ends meet. Without any ideological traces of political ambitions, he succeeds in giving an intense picture of the deep United States, less touched by cameras, news reports and TV reportage. In the stories he tells, one feels touches of the cinema of John Cassavetes and Robert Altman, Wim Wenders and the *New American Cinema*, of early Martin Scorsese (think of the masterpieces *Mean Streets* and *Taxi Driver*), between marginalisation and misery, stubbornness and alcohol. But more often than not, his characters are terribly and simply average,

---

8   G. Nocera, *Cronologia*, in Raymond Carver, *Racconti*, Mondadori, Milan 2005, p. 50.

ordinary, without any apparent positive or negative vicissitudes. Flat calm in provincial horizons, among human shadows worthy of Edward Hopper's paintings, George Segal's sculptures, the songs of Lou Reed, Ricky Lee Jones and Tom Waits. Orality, after all, has been of great importance in American literature since the mid-19th century.[9]

Fundamental to understanding the different facets of such a complex human and artistic persona as Carver's is the long 1986 interview granted to the Paris Review. In a central passage, the writer explains, or rather recounts, why he always measures himself with the short story form instead of the novel form. It is a matter of extraliterary motivations, such as the circumstances that accompany writing: he needs both material to be finished quickly (between main jobs that have nothing to do with literature) and works that make him money immediately. When he then has the merit (but also the luck) to take on university lectures, magazine assignments and various writing grants, he will calibrate himself to the measure of tales rather than novels or romance. In the late 1960s and early 1980s, alcoholism also prevented him from dedicating himself to the novel - so much so that he came to describe himself as a 'full-time career drunkard' for a long time.

Let us dwell on the decisive pages in which he recounts (as always, rather than explains) how he writes, narrating his day as a craftsman of stories.

The days fit into each other when he manages to work on a collection for the whole week and the following week until he has finished. When he teaches, however, he spends the time he has left over from the course or the seminary waiting for the right moment to resume writing; and he knows that that moment comes, sooner or later. If he is at the typewriter, he is able to hold out for 12 or 15 hours a day, especially for the re-writing and revision work for

---

9 "The familiar, digressive American voice, then, bears all the marks of living matter; it is rough, worn, ragged, full of smoke, whiskey, sand and gravel - it is the voice of Louis Armstrong and Little Richard (...) of Tom Waits and Bob Dylan and Lenny Bruce. That is why it is capable of (...) condensing to the edges", *Oralità e scrittura negli Stati Uniti*, in F. Moretti (ed.), *Il romanzo. Volume terzo: Storia e geografia*, Einaudi, Turin 2002, p. 437.

which he is justifiably famous during his lifetime. Poems, perhaps even more so than short stories, he is never in a hurry to send them to publishers, preferring to keep them at home for months at a time, perhaps without doing more work on them than that. The versions of the short stories are never less than 10-12, but can reach more than 30. And when he finds his own first drafts of a short story or poem horrible, he consoles himself by thinking of Tolstoy, a painstaking reviser, as obstinate and obsessive as Carver.

Let us read a long quotation from a passage that is illuminating in its semi-descriptiveness about the author's method of craftsmanship in *Cathedral*:

> I throw down the first draft pretty quickly. Most of the time I do this by hand. I stand there and fill pages and pages as quickly as possible. In some cases I use a kind of personal shorthand, I even make notes to myself to remind myself of things I will have to do when I get back to it. Certain scenes I have to leave unfinished, sometimes even unwritten, these are the scenes that will require meticulous care later on. I mean, it is clear that everything requires meticulous care - it is just that I put certain scenes aside and do not develop them until the second or third draft, because it would take me too long in the first draft to do them well. The first draft serves me to get the story down in broad strokes, to build a kind of scaffolding. Then, in subsequent versions, I will think about adding the rest. When I have finished the hand draft, I type a version of the story and start reworking that. It feels like a different story, it naturally improves after I type it. When I type it the first time, I already start to rewrite, to add or remove here and there. But the real work begins later, after I have typed two or three different drafts. The same happens with poems, only poems can have as many as thirty or forty drafts.[10]

There are numerous aspects that are striking in this description: painstaking dedication, infinite patience, the ability to see the conclusion as the final task as it is finally defined. There is no risk of exhaustion; on the contrary, it is only by exhausting all possible mixtures, arrangements, balancing of words and sentences that one can arrive at the final draft.

---

10   R. Carver, *Intervista*, Minimum Fax, Rome 1996, pp. 34-35.

The other aspect that makes Carver's 'writing workshop work' quite special, apart from the one just seen of rewrites - in a hellish but ultimately magical circle of creative obsessiveness - is the subtraction, the 'take away' part of the matter from the whole matter, leaving what is needed, the right one. And what is right is made up of very delicate balances, almost like a pharmacist weighing the micrograms more or less on the balance, avoiding reducing the medicine to poison or immiserating it into an ineffective substance.

How much of what he writes does he end up definitively discarding?

Quite a lot. If the first draft of a story is forty pages long, it is usually reduced to at least half that length by the time I have finished reworking it. And it's not just a question of removing or reducing. I take out a lot of things, but I also add a lot of things and then I add more and take out more. It's something I really enjoy doing, adding and taking words out of a story.[11]

In this passage, it is inevitable to highlight the childlike playfulness of *homo ludens* analysed by Huizinga.[12]

The apprenticeship took place between the end of the 1950s and the early 1960s, when the sawmill worker, writer, university student at alternate times, young husband, very young father (barely 20 years of age or slightly older) set out on the road that gave glory and fame to Hemingway and Fitzgerald in the 1920s, as well as Salinger in the 1950s. He published in the best magazines of the American literary twentieth century, the same as the aforementioned colleagues who preceded him: "Harper's Bazar" and "Collier's", "Atlantic" and "Esquire", not to mention the most modernising and prestigious of them all, "New Yorker". Rayond Carver's name, after all, appears relatively late, with an agonising wait, which other writers do not have to endure - think, for one name among all, of the precocious talent of Truman Capote. In this sense, it is a 'long apprenticeship' - to paraphrase the ironic title (since he is also quite precocious) of the collection of short stories edited by Thomas Pynchon.

---

11   Ibid, pp. 37-38.
12   J. Huizinga, *Homo ludens. Il gioco come funzione sociale*, Il Saggiatore, Milan 1967, in particular chapters *Natura e significato del gioco come fenomeno culturale, Gioco e poesia* and *Forme ludiche dell'arte*.

The training (the craftsman's workshop seems like a gymnasium), the art of 'toiling' to achieve supreme conciseness, the spread of creative writing courses in so many colleges and universities in those years, as well as the wealth of menial jobs and odd jobs that Carver does tirelessly during the day (writing and studying at night) are the very solid basis, as the years go by, on which the absolutely unique and original by this maniac (in the best sense) of 'cutting and stitching' sentences within the short story form.

He wants to decisively precisely change this form that has made literature in the United States of America great for several decades now. And he succeeds in doing so in relatively few years, fully aware of the need to grow and of the time to be fruitfully employed in the maturation of literary craftsmanship. On the one hand, he keeps his distance from the fashions of the moment (think first of all of the post-modernism of a John Barth or a Donald Barthelme, as well as of Pynchon himself); while on the other hand, he has no particular contiguity with the rising tide of minimalism, the authorship of which is hastily - and therefore superficially - attributed to him. We refer to Susan Minot and Gundula Janowitz, David Leavitt and Amy Hempel, Brett Easton Ellis and Jay Mc Inerney.[13]

It should be borne in mind that this renewal of the short story form as part of the renewal of American literature between the 1960s and 1980s - overseen by Carver - cannot fail to have reverberations in terms of the modification of the ethical level of literary communication, of an enrichment of new values for every reader who comes face to face with the dozens of short stories that come out of Carver's workshop over the years. Indeed, as Cesare Segre writes in one of the introductory pages to a fundamental text for literary studies in the second half of the 20th century:

> Given an author or a behaviour, it is a question of identifying and naming its ethical motivations; then, since the characters and behaviours

---

13   For two different and equally stimulating approaches to literature in the USA, see: L. Briasco and M. Carratello (eds.), *La letteratura americana dal 1900 a oggi. Dizionario per autori*, Einaudi, Turin 2011; C. Scarpino, C. Schiavini, S.M. Zangari, *Guida alla letteratura degli Stati Uniti. Percorsi e protagonisti 1945- 2014*, Odoya, Bologna 2014.

are inserted into an action that they mostly determine or undergo, it is necessary to grasp the deductions suggested by the reciprocal relationship (...) the reader (...) is therefore pushed to critically examine the moral or behavioural foundations of the characters and conceive mediations or theoretical overcoming that change the framework of current ideas (...) is therefore prompted to critically examine the moral or behavioural foundations of the characters and to conceive of mediations or theoretical overcoming that change the framework of current ideas (...) The literary work is thus seen above all in its ability to renew the tables of values, the meaning of life.[14]

Then, at a certain point along the way, Carver arrives at a kind of degree zero (to paraphrase Roland Barthes) as the definitive point of arrival. The painstaking excavation in the form, the removal of the superfluous, the gradual conquest of a writing that is increasingly rarefied as much as it is rich in details, even the tiniest ones, arrive at the maximum of possibility and meaning. A point that Nocera makes very clear in his precious introductory essay to the Meridiano Mondadori dedicated to all of Carveri's short stories:

> his energy as an 'instinctive writer', his lack of imagination make him realise that on the path from Desolation Angels to What do we talk about when we talk about love, it is precisely that very writing that has been iconised in surgical terms as reduced to the bone, and which has brought him so much success, that has also made him border on a kind of degree zero of narration, beyond which it is not possible to proceed.[15]

---

14   C. Segre, *Introduzione all'edizione italiana*, in W. Iser, *L'atto della lettura. Una teoria della risposta estetica*, Il Mulino, Bologna 1987, p. 20. The comparison with another of the greatest literary scholars of the same period, with very different perspectives, is very stimulating: 'How does the graft take hold of our being? What is it that transforms the momentary reception (the knocks at the door) - even when this reception is involuntary, subliminal, hostile, since there are many images, melodies, evocations that we would gladly get rid of - into a lasting residence? The honest answer is that we do not know'. G. Steiner, *Vere presenze*, Garzanti, Milan 1998, p. 173.

15   Nocera, *L'America profonda di Raymond Carver*, in Carver, *Tutti i racconti...*, cit., p. XXVII.

PART III
ROADS TO ANOTHER AMERICA
Roth, Auster, Wallace, Franzen

1
INTRODUCTION ON THE 1970S-1990S

The population of the United States between 1940 and 1980 increased by as much as 95 million to 226 million the year before Ronald Reagan came to power. But part of that figure is due to emigration, which continues to bring in hundreds of thousands of people every year. The trend that continues to this day - bringing the population to as many as 320 million in the 1910s - thus originated even before the start of World War II.

In addition to the constant increase in the number of inhabitants, problems relating to integration, and the phenomenon of illegal immigrants (starting with the *caliente* border with Mexico), there are also difficulties linked to the profound industrial, technological, and economic changes and the consequences in the organisation of society. The urban crisis gives rise to phenomena such as the development of deprived neighbourhoods (the slums), the insecurity experienced in large cities such as New York and Chicago, Los Angeles, and Washington, with increasing common crime and the presence of mafias from countries such as China and Japan, Mexico and Italy. From the 1960s we inherit the war in faraway Vietnam, the greatest US disaster on many different levels: more than 50,000 dead, around 2 million local civilians killed, the indiscriminate use of defoliants and napalm bombs, as well as torture; the country's international image ruined and patriotic sentiment swept under the carpet, along with the immense costs for a war that cynics call 'useless, indeed harmful'.

Youth changes profoundly: it moves between the crisis of national tradition and the profound criticism of the *American Way of Life*, libertarian spirit, and counterculture in the 1970s; then it slides in the following decade towards the triumph of money and the death of ideology, social egoism and the race for unbridled wealth, the cult of the body and mistrust of non-conformist cultures and criticism of western models. Reagan for two terms in office and Bush sr. for one led the States along an exaltation of the wealthy class and of individual and family commitment to ever greater prosperity. The concept of aid to emerging countries is attacked, the affairs of poor areas in Central and South America are more influenced than in the past, as well as the Far East, supporting pro-American warriors and terrorists who sabotage the left's attempts at self-government - think Nicaragua or El Salvador.

Domestically, trade unions are discouraged and hindered in every way, strikes are equated with criminal acts, while the sharp reduction of taxation on the upper classes is legitimised, gigantic privatisation projects of public services are launched, and the activities of the arms lobby (the National Rifle Association) are encouraged.

What emerges is the image (and substance) of a neo-imperial, aggressive and fiercely anti-communist America abroad, linked inseparably to Margareth Thatcher's Great Britain.

Internally, morality is centred on the cult of the individual, the new hero of the frontier of prosperity and the greatest possible wealth. While those who suffer from poverty and marginalisation, psychological distress or alcohol and drug consumption (but not if they belong to the privileged classes), or lead an alternative existence, linked to countercultures or to contestation and voluntary work, are condemned as the 'sole cause of their own evil'.

The model of aggressive and hyper-egoistic late capitalism is extolled, while solidarity and open-mindedness and cultural openness are dismissed as 19th-century ironclad. In turn, the vision of the interventionist state in economy, a moderate regulator of market follies and distortions, structured to support those in need of help with the Roosevelt-era welfare edifice, is deeply despised and the structures systematically dismantled. Those who are rich or do everything to become so are the good citizens, while those who are not or do not behave this way are marginalised. Naturally, the darker the skin, the greater the likelihood of finding oneself in the lowest strata of society. The vast majority of the more than two million inmates are in fact African American, Oriental or Central and South American.

A contemporary historian writes:

> In this theoretically classless society, there remained an enormous inequality between the rich and the poor. According to the poverty line drawn by the Census Bureau (...) the proportion of Americans living in poverty had fallen from 22% in 1959 to 11% in 1974; however, this meant that more than twenty-five million people were officially classified as poor. Moreover, the percentage of national income accruing to the poorest 20% of the population had remained relatively constant since 1870.[1]

Literature reflects these profound changes and cannot be otherwise. The mirror of the social that is art often turns dark, losing some of the serenity and constructive anger that marked the period between the mid- fifties and early seventies, when one moves between *beatniks* and *hippies*, counterculture and protest, humanistic hopes and escapes to India or Nepal.

But do not think that the creative horizon is reduced to a corner, silent and almost offended with the course of history. Read what the authors of a successful handbook of literary history write:

> These were the years of reflux, of collective withdrawal, of the reduction of problems to purely private and individual dimensions, of the tendency to fragment and anaesthetise reality, of the predominance, in the collective imagination and in its forms and manifestations, of the world of the stock market, fashion, television and advertising. But (...) subterranean tensions, mute or explicit disaffection, dissatisfaction and discomfort are felt (...).[2]

The development of women's consciousness and the homosexual/lesbian question, the spread of a green and environmental culture, massive immigration from more and more distant countries and cultures, the spread of alphabetisation and rising levels of education, rap and graffiti cultures from the ghettos, the emergence of artists literally from the street - from Haring to Basquiat - and minimalist musicians (Glass, Riley, Reich), the photography of Mapplethorpe,

---

1   Jones, *Storia degli Stati Uniti...*, cit., pp. 528-29.
2   Fink, Maffi, Minganti, Tarozzi, *Storia della letteratura...*, cit., p. 533.

urban poets and musicians à la Lou Reed and Patty Smith are just a few examples of stubborn presences, critical of the consumerist, egoistic, hyper-bourgeois and warmongering trend of official America.

If one criticises the excesses of the novelists of the minimalist current, one realises, however, that names such as Bret Easton Ellis, Jay McInerney and David Leavitt can portray the family and its sorrows, the world of business, fashion, and entertainment with often iconoclastic force as horizons of depersonalising emptiness and perverse idiocy. Attempts are made to dismiss a masterpiece such as *American Psycho* by passing it off as a scandalous and perverse book, whereas it is much more difficult to contest it in its truth as a dark mirror of the Reagan hedonist era.[3]

But alongside minimalism and its alleged adherents - think of the equivocal about Raymond Carver, who has almost nothing to do with this group, even though he partly inspired it - we find the dense school of post-modernism: Thomas Pynchon, who is perhaps its most respected representative, Kurt Vonnegut and Donald Barthelme, John Barth and Richard Brautigan. But their field of research often produces such a level of experimentation that they are known almost exclusively to literary experts and particularly educated readers.

Other 'families' of novelists congregate around New Age conceptions, between pacifism, Orientalism, and green thinking; or science fiction, thrillers and mysteries - from Ursula Le Guin to Philip Dick, to the celebrated and hyper-prolific Stephen King, who has so far sold more than half a billion copies of the seventy or so volumes he has written.

In any case, the novel form stubbornly persists, despite all the recurring funeral declarations in its honour, the new technologies that threaten the printed page, and the increasing distraction for

---

3   "The novelist John Barth wrote in 1986 in *Brevi note sul minimalismo*, somewhat clumsily attempting to map this current as famous as it is misunderstood: 'silent' removal of the Vietnam trauma, reaction to the American culture of excess and waste, decline of literacy - a widely debated theme in the United States (...) and the practice of reading, reaction towards the high intellectual density fabulation of the various Barth, Gass, Barthelme (...)'. Pynchon. Fink, Maffi, Minganti, Tarozzi, *Storia della letteratura...*, cit., p. 549.

adolescents and young people constituted first by TV, then by computer media. As the aforementioned Fink and colleagues write:

> The novel thus refuses extinction, accepts those limits, the exceeding of which had entailed risks and accusations of illegibility (...) and reaffirms its own identity by questioning the functions of storytelling, resizing and deconstructing rules and codes, and openly exposing, *in corpore vili*, the innumerable cultural conventions of intertextual functioning.[4]

---

4   Ibid, p. 539.

2
PHILIP ROTH

2.1 Defending the faith. The first Roth scandal

The most paradigmatic case of failure to win a Nobel Prize for literature (we sincerely hope to be proven wrong at the next award ceremony) is also the one who is considered by many authoritative critics to be the most significant living writer.

> 'Give Philip Roth the Nobel Prize to honour his retirement': nothing. Even the application of intellectuals on the other side of the ocean that the British Telegraph had picked up went unheeded by academic ears.[1]

Philip Roth happily freed himself from writing three years before his eightieth birthday (celebrated in '13), to devote himself to reading and friends, music, and freedom from the passion/joy of the stories he told readers between 1959 and 2010. In a beautiful and rare interview, he explains how he sees the characters and their dialogue:

> A fictional character comes to life through what they say and what they do not say; it is one of the means the novelist uses. Dialogue is an expression of their thoughts, beliefs, defences, wit, exchanges of banter, etc., in general a depiction of how they react.[2]

Far from a repudiation of what he has done in half a century of literary creation or a nostalgic rethinking of the word 'end' put on

---

1   A. Aquaro, *Roth attacca il Nobel: 'Sono dei provinciali'*, La Repubblica quotidiano, 19 January 2013.

2   P. Roth, *'Che bella la vita quando non devi più passarla a scrivere'*. *Intervista* di Cynthia Haven, The Daily Republic, 22 February 2014.

his 32 books, Roth's decision at 77 to devote himself to something else has the flavour of a serene *devoir accompli*, as the French say.[3]

To get an idea of how in literature tout se tient, in the sense of the circularity of a theme, an object/subject, an event involving one, a hundred, a million people, the South African Nobel laureate Coetzee lucidly traces a concise echo that has the treatment (in the artistic sense) of the reality of contagious diseases, or supposedly so, from Defoe's Irish 1600s to the 1900s in two different moments: Camus's 1940s France and Roth's latest romance released in 2010 but set in 1944 New York. The story is the same in reality (Coetzee recalls the 19,000 cases of poliomyelitis in the U.S.A. that year) as much as it is told differently by different writers - as it should be, being literature:

> The psychopathology of populations under attack by diseases whose transmission is ill understood was explored by Daniel Defoe in his *Journal of the Plague Year*, which pretends to be the journal of a survivor of the bubonic plague that decimated London in 1655. (...) Albert Camus knew Defoe's *Journal*: in his novel *The Plague*, written during the war years, he quotes from it and generally imitates the matter-of-fact tone of Defoe's narrator towards the catastrophe unfolding around him. (...)

In a 2008 interview, Philip Roth mentioned that he had been rereading *The Plague*. Now he has published Nemesis, set in Newark in the polio summer of 1944 (19,000 cases nationwide).[4]

The perception of his own talent mixed with an intense desire, a r e a l urge to write, led a 26-year-old to stir up a bitter controversy within the strict and orthodox Jewish community in and around Newark (at least in the neighbouring states of New Jersey and New York). The stone of scandal is Roth's first book, a short novel followed by a collection of five short stories, published in 1959 under the title

---

3   "I no longer have the strength to bear the frustration. Writing is a frustration, a daily frustration, not to mention humiliation (...) I can no longer imagine spending any more days where you write five pages and throw them away. I can't do it anymore'. P. Roth, *'Perché è finita la mia lotta con la scrittura'. Intervista* di Carles McGrath, La Repubblica quotidiano, 19 November 2012.
4   J.M. Coetzee, *On the Moral Brink. Philip Roth*, Nemesis, The New York Review of Books, 28 October 2010.

Goodbye, Columbus. And *Five Short Stories*. More precisely, it is a short story, *Defender of the Faith*, that triggers the reprimands of certain Jewish figures in the great New England states.[5]

The author was stunned by the scandal, which was also heightened by another account in the collection, *Conversion of the Jews*. Today, 55 years later, the controversy appears in all its speciousness and 'prudery religious'. As critic Claudia Roth Pierpont (no relation to the writer) well points out, it is the possibility of characters like those described by Roth and the publication of the story in a goy (gentile, non-Jewish) weekly like The New Yorker that are the real reasons for the controversy. A rabbi wrote to Roth himself explaining that if it had appeared in a Jewish publication and in Hebrew, the story would have been a short story, therefore to be judged literally; but its appearance in a 'gentile' weekly became nothing more than a mere informative note (therefore completely *politically uncorrect*, one would say today):

> In fact, "your story - in Hebrew - in an Israeli magazine or newspaper", the censorious rabbi wrote to Roth, "would have been judged exclusively from a literary point of view". Here, however, in America, in a magazine widely esteemed in Gentile society, Roth's best efforts amounted to nothing less than an act of 'informing'".[6]

But the 'first good work I ever wrote' - as the author makes clear in those months - shows the inability of the Jewish community, some fifteen years after the end of the war and the Shoah, to face its demons. One thinks of the intolerability, for many in the community, of what the student of *Conversion of the Jews* says to his rabbi, noting the jarring contradiction between the equality of all human beings according to the US *Declaration of Independence*, and the conception of the Jews as the Chosen People.[7]

---

5   P. Roth, *Difensore della fede*, in *Goodbye, Columbus*, Einaudi, Turin 2012, pp. 135-168.

6   C. Pierpont Roth, *Roth Unbound. A man and his books*, Jonathan Cape 2013, p. 9.

7   P. Roth, *La conversione degli Ebrei*, in *Goodbye, Columbus*, Einaudi, Turin 2012, pp. 118-134. What the American literary critic Matthiessen wrote in the 1940s seems very appropriate in this context: writers whose need was to start

Roth refrains from tackling an extremely burning subject that a few years later contributed to ruining Hannah Arendt's health with t h e publication of her famous report on the Eichmann trial. For a short time, the writer plans to tell a story about the existence of the Jewish councils, the notorious *Judenräte*, which in many cases helped to bring about the extermination of their own people by helping the Germans from an organisational point of view.[8]

But he agrees to take the advice of those who ask him to desist because it is too early to deal with such a hot topic; and the terrible *querelle* unleashed against Arendt will confirm this between 1963 and '66.[9]

It is Roth himself who recalls how the collective memory of pogroms and the Shoah marks the Jews' self-awareness of their own value, as well as their distinction as a people who

> consisted in the *inability* to perpetrate bloodshed such as our ancestors had suffered.[10]

Jewishness is a given ('as peaceful as having two arms and two legs'), the writer recounts in the autobiographical volume *The Facts*, which, however, does not detract from being as American as all other *goym* compatriots. The parents of young Philip, his cousins and neighbourhood friends, on the other hand, mark the generational distance, coming from European families where Yiddish (the typical half-Jewish, half-German dialect used in the territories of Eastern European Jewry, between Poland, Galicia, Ukraine, and Russia,

---

afresh. What they had to say did not fit conventional taste because it was often anguished matter: it was often an acute conflict between exteriority and interiority F.O. Matthiessen, *Le responsabilità del critico*, Feltrinelli, Milan 1966, p. 123.

8   On this topic see R. Hilberg, *La distruzione degli Ebrei d'Europa*, 2 volumes, Einaudi, Turin 1995, § *Le Vittime*, pp. 1110-1124. On the controversy surrounding the German philosopher I refer to R. D'Alessandro, *La pensatrice e lo specialista. Hannah Arendt e il processo Eichmann*, Ombre Corte, Verona 2015.

9   "To elaborate - as the intellectual must do - an alternative thought to the dominant conventions, which kill, dehumanise and rationalise the human spirit". E. Said, *Sullo stile tardo*, Il Saggiatore, Milan 2009, p. 128.

10   P. Roth, *I fatti. Autobiografia di un romanziere*, Leonardo, Milan 1989, p. 32.

the so-called *Ostjudentum*) is still spoken. So, the grandparents remained Eastern European Jews, the children are already half integrated in the States, the children's children are 100% American. An unbridgeable distance therefore marks Philip and his parents:

> As unaccented as they spoke English, as secular as they were, as convincing as their American way of life was, our parents were nevertheless conditioned by their childhood upbringing and were still bound by ancestral ties to what to us, the children of the second generation, seemed antiquated customs and outdated concepts.[11]

2.2 *Writer or pornographer? The Portnoy complex*

It is probable that, as connoisseurs of the subject, called upon to collect Philip Roth's best pages, his alter egos would extract from the books in which they themselves are protagonists the pages in which their creator's sarcasm resonates loudest, and at the same time all the passages into which he poured his most private obsessions: the stereotype of the miserable petty-bourgeois Jew, sexual greed, the terror of illness and death.[12]

The reflection of the cultural contributor to 'Il Manifesto' applies very well to the most famous of Roth's many characters; and we would add 'undeservedly famous', thinking only of Mickey Sabbath, perhaps the best told of Roth's more than thirty characters.

---

11   Roth, *I fatti...*, cit., p. 35. It is interesting to read what the Americanist Claudio
        Gorlier writes: 'the Jew knows from the outset that he is *something else* twice
        over: an alienated individual par excellence in an alienated society (...) the
        appropriation of certain great American idols - success, money, the centrality
        of the family unit - acquires macroscopic dimensions, because it is set in terms
        of a revenge: for an American Jew who is proud of himself and faithful to the
        spirit of the clan, the 'New York Times' acquires the significance of a shrine,
        a symbol of the success of a dynasty of co-religionists (...) But alongside the
        idols, at least in appearance positive, other idols are appropriated, starting
        with the mortification of the sex peculiar to a country prone to the exercise,
        puritanical or Victorian, or both, of repression'.
        C. Gorlier, *Introduzione*, in P. Roth, *Il lamento di Portnoy*, Bompiani, Milan 1970,
        p. 6.
12   F. Borrelli, *Provaci ancora Roth*, Alias Sunday-supplement to Il Manifesto,
        daily newspaper, 18 November 2012.

It may seem strange that at the very beginning of his literary career, the two scandals related, as seen, to *Goodbye, Columbus* (limited to the two short stories mentioned) and ten years later to *Portnoy's Lament* are produced. After a few less successful books, Roth's case takes off with the long season of mature masterpieces; but no more *quarrels* are produced. Precisely by virtue of the same society described by the author, which in the meantime has evolved, disengaged itself from late-Victorian prudery thanks to the sexual revolution and youth movements in Western countries. A society that has simultaneously secularised itself through the process of secularisation, intertwined in turn with the spread of capitalist democracy. In the light of these far-reaching transformations that took place between the 1960s and 1980s, the resignation of a couple of years ago from the jury of an important British prize by a literary critic is worthy of its justification: Roth, who had just been awarded the prize by that jury, was unworthy of the award because he had 'mistreated' the female characters in his novels. From inquisitorial and moralistic censure, we have thus come to the mystifications of angry and ignorant pseudo-feminists.[13]

But the scandal of 1959 and that of ten years later differ on several fronts. If the former was born and died out almost in the narrow milieu of orthodox New England Jewry, the latter filled North American, then European newspapers and magazines.

Moreover, one revolves around religious issues, while the other revolves around sexual and ethical (or allegedly so) issues.

Thirdly, while the 26-year old newcomer soon douses his head in black, promising the Jewish religious authorities that he would no longer deal with *jewishness* in his future works (an oath which, fortunately, he will be careful not to keep), 1969 sees a man who is still young but already mature, who faces the fame and wealth that *Portnoy*'s remarkable sales bring him with astonished joy: Suffice it to say that with the proceeds he buys himself a new car, settles his

---

13   An antecedent to this is a sharp piece that appeared in 1976 in the quintessential radical US weekly, *The Village Voice*, by Vivian Gornick, which lumps together allegedly macho writers such as Roth and Henry Miller, Bellow and Mailer. Pierpont, *Roth Unbound*, cit., p. 81.

debts and negotiates the purchase of a much larger and more elegant house on New York's East Side.[14]

Fourthly, the remembered sexual revolution, which matured from the mid-1960s onwards and which started in the United States and spread throughout the industrialised West, is the ideal sea in which any scandal, like the Rothian novel, is destined to turn into other water that nourishes that sea in which moralists soon drown.

In reality, however, it is not the case to speak of a Roth interested in political and/or moral subversion. An Italian critic rightly observes that his characters desire two things above all: social integration and women. While the former is to be conquered with an interesting, economically and socially recognised job (no Rothian character is a plumber or unemployed!), women, on the other hand, are possessed less by true love than by passion and erotic involvement. As the years go by, then, the narrative horizon becomes much darker, completely dispelling any suspicion of radical political commitment in the author (suffice it to mention a book like Everyman, an undisputed masterpiece).[15]

But what does the writer say about his most famous book? He speaks of an exploit of hard work that brings to light his fourth work, completely different from his previous ones, both in terms of 'exuberance' and the story it tells. It is inspired by the actual psychoanalysis carried out by Roth; but at the same time, he himself considers the novel much more entertaining and free than the treatment he undertook.

One can speak of at least three paths of liberation realised with *The Portnoy Chin*: from Jewishness, from the weight of certain literary traditions - he names James and Flaubert - and again from the psychoanalytic commitment that is reread with lightness and irony in the course of the protagonist's story.

What had started as an exaggerated and unfaithful transcription of a psychoanalytic monologist who could also have been my own, then diverging from mine more and more due to the obvious hyperbole and the bizarre and mythical atmosphere created by the farcical

---

14   Pierpont, *Roth Unbound*, cit., p. 62.
15   See L. De Fiore, *Roth. Fantasmi del desiderio*, Editori Riuniti, Rome 2012, in particular pp. 8-9.

invention about the profane trinity of Jewish father, mother and son, had gradually turned into an all-round comic counter-analysis.[16]

---

16   Roth, *I fatti...*, cit., p. 150. Let us also read what Martin Amis, Roth's admirer and colleague, writes, capturing some central aspects of the 1969 novel: what the reader was looking for, then, was a novel that only Philip Roth could have written. "That novel was *Portnoy's Lament* (1969) - a biting, cackling comedy, a time bomb (explosive even typographically, so much so that it set the overall record, in mainstream fiction, for exclamation marks, capital letters and italics). In it, the tensions and conflicts of the Jewish-American experience are reduced to their core: the shiksa (non-Jewish girls). The yjddish root of the word means 'detested object': in patrilineal logic, goy males are tolerable, but shiksa mean assimilation and are therefore forbidden. Forbidden, detested - and all the more strongly desired. Roth attacked this crucial point with unparalleled energy; it seemed as if that turbulent, directionless talent had finally found a perfect pitch'. M. Amis, *Il mio Roth. L'uomo che fa di se stesso un romanzo*, La Repubblica, daily, 20 November 2013.

3
SITTING IN A ROOM, ALL ALONE.
AUSTER WRITER

If any aspiring writer is convinced that publishers' rejections are only worth it for him, he can think of many distant and recent cases of countless attempts before succeeding in appearing in bookshops and on the third pages of newspapers (when third pages still existed). Paul Auster, for instance, suffered 17 rejections for *City of Glass* before he managed to publish it in 1987. But he says he was 'born a writer, a desperate case who can do nothing else'. At the cost of reaching the limits of minimum sufficient living, like having difficulty literally putting a meal a day in his stomach. His negative, exclusionary self-awareness is very clear, pro- grammatic: he does not know how to do anything else, does not want to do anything else, has never done anything else, and never will do anything else - confirmation, if any were needed, of the strength of character required to write (as well as to perform music or compose it, act or direct films, theatre plays, paint, sculpt).

The experience that marks him most in terms of literary heritage is Dostoevsky's, in particular *Crime and Punishment*, the reading of which gave him such a powerful experience that he wanted to write for the rest of his life and make it his own work.

Writing is not a very interesting way to live: sitting all day in a club, all alone, concentrating on a typewriter. Yet I could not imagine not doing it: my life would be empty and incomplete if I did not write.[1]

Being a writer thus becomes a dimension of existence in itself (decided by the spirit), not comparable to a conceptual job, manual trade, freelance profession. One renounces (willingly or unwillingly)

---

1   P. Auster, *Le trame della scrittura. Intervista* di Matteo Bellinelli, Casagrande, Lugano 2005, p. 30.

the socialisation offered/imposed by an office, building site, shop, or professional studio. This is also why so many novelists (excluding agoraphobic or asocial incurables) like to present their books in public, discuss with readers, sign copies (even hundreds of them), to experience the socialisation dimension, they renounce precisely because of the very special activity they so desperately want to perform.

The book-interview just mentioned is one of the most direct and interesting testimonies, able to let us enter the craft workshop of one of the contemporary American writers among the most appreciated by the public and stymied by the critics. After all, volumes of this kind - an all- round interview at a high level, without being a programmatic and intellectualistic 'brick' - are much rarer than one might think. What is more, Auster is a special case, considering that he writes novels, short stories, articles on cultural and current affairs journalism, film scripts, often engages in awareness-raising campaigns on environmental and political issues, as well as being the husband of a talented fellow novelist Siri Hustvedt (of Norwegian origin, naturalised US). More than once, they have shown themselves to be a very solid couple, in relation to her depressive problems and their mutual closeness and solidarity in writing.

What Auster explains about autobiography in the contemporary novel is very interesting:

> Although I am not an autobiographical writer, I have very rarely used elements of my life in my novels, only a few things here and there. Naturally, I am much more present in my essays and nonfiction texts. But the process of writing certainly interests me a lot, and I have always wanted to make it an integral part of a book. Perhaps it is an element of naivety that I have been carrying around since I was a boy. I mean you pick up a novel, and it is usually written in the third person. For example, by Charles Dickens. So you read a voice, but you don't really know whose it is. Is it Charles Dickens', is it the author's, is it the authorial voice of Charles Dickens? Who witnessed the events recounted in the novel? God, perhaps? Or who else? And how does he know all these things?[2]

---

2   Auster, *Le trame della scrittura...*, cit., p. 32.

The comparison with the Creator of the world and humanity is a constant: think of the perfection of the circle drawn freehand by Giotto or Mozart's compositional ability, the devilry that Paganini or Liszt are able to pull out of their respective instruments and the grandeur of Balzac's work. But for Auster, when the character telling the story enters the story itself, helping the readers to verify the information, then it is precisely the kind of novel he loves to write and does in fact write.

Another aspect of being a writer for months, years, decades is the loneliness it necessarily entails, while each new book is a question mark that comes out (when it comes out) exclusively from within the author, not being the result of group work, workshop, editorial staff, department. Certainly, there are many lonelinesses that one experiences while working: but how particular is that of one who wants to invent stories, and since becoming a writer, the *desire* also becomes a *duty* - for oneself, the public, the agent, the publisher, the critics. A loneliness but constantly threatened by reproaches, rejections, disinterest, complaints, competition with other talents.

For the New Yorker writer, ideas guide him as they are processed and produced, but the form of the story comes of its own accord - in other words, 'literary material finds its own form'.

When it comes to fusing story and characters, dialogue, and description, with the carat of language Auster is constantly searching for the good sound of sentences, the appropriate sound. And here we are close to the sensitivity for music of an East Coast North American, also from New York, educated in Paris, a lover of classical, jazz and pop. One thinks of his collaborations with Lou Reed (former Velvet Underground), Madonna and John Lurie in the film *Blue in the Face*, the follow-up to *Smoke*.[3]

The very act of creating, a continuous gesture and yet one that is continually at risk (the terror of the blank page, today more often than not the blank PC screen) leads, says the author of *Oracle Night*, almost to living as if in society. He tries to understand its meaning, perhaps mentally ruminating on its contents, its obscure aspects

---

3   For the critical entries on the two films see P. Mereghetti, *Dizionario dei film 2011*, Baldini Castoldi Dalai, Milan 2010, respectively vol. A-L, pp. 461-62 and vol. M-Z, pp. 3117-18.

even for years, before the project for a new book emerges from it. Here, intensity and doubts, slow processing times (rather than drafting, considering Auster's large number of published works), amnestic traces and a psychoanalytic approach are mixed together - in a land where Freudian analysis has been 'de-orthodoxised' and contaminated, often in ways that are entirely banal and prone to the way of life in a society as mass- capitalist as that of the United States.

The only necessity is our end, which awaits us inevitably; while what lies between birth and death, Auster considers philosophically, is a combination of chance and will. Thus, living is caught between these two elements, but it also offers us freedom and the ability to plan. Although the author of *Being and Nothingness* is not mentioned, the influence of existentialist thought and culture in the French and particularly Sartrian version. There is a real 'music of chance', says the New York-based writer, which weaves together both real and fictional life.

His studies at Columbia University in the second half of the 1960s represented a cultural and mental experience of great importance, considering the musical and countercultural richness, as well as the era of youth protest and the fight against the Vietnam War.

But the three and a half years spent in Paris over the next decade are perhaps Auster's most intense school of life at the turn of the twenties. It is not for nothing that the first texts he finds satisfying come during the period when he has just returned from the French capital, when he finally feels ready to step out into American and then world literary life. The many jobs he held in his youth often kept him away from his desk while helping him discover the world. Hence, literature is above all the telling of people, places, situations that one gains valuable experience of by being in the world. Perhaps even better where another language is spoken, another culture breathed, immersing oneself in the complex and rich world. Only then will Paul Auster be able to tell New York like few others.

4
FOSTER WALLACE

4.1 *Giving something to the reader. The idea of writing in Foster Wallace*

A young man of exceptional literary ability, gifted in non-fiction, mathematics, and logic, versed in philosophy and an excellent tennis player, an accomplished teacher of creative writing and the history of literature, a loving father and mother, esteemed by his colleagues, a friend of De Lillo and Franzen, committed suicide at the age of 46, in 1998, after half of his adult life spent battling depression. His name is David Foster Wallace.

Here is a vivid description of it dating back to 1987:

> The class taught by Wallace - English 210, 'Introduction to Fiction Writing' - is about to begin. (...) Tall and pale, thin as a stick and with a stunted stubble, David wears a red-striped Brooksgate shirt with long sleeves and buttons at the collar, and a pair of half-unlaced hunter's Timber-lands: probably the only pair of shoes of its kind in the entire University of Arizona. (...) David leads the workshop with the professionalism of a veteran, dissecting, clarifying, pointing out the shortcomings of the stories and their strengths. (...) Witty, engaging, profound and illuminating.[1]

For David Foster Wallace, writing is inseparable from reflecting on what and when one writes. And what is better than reflecting aloud, gathering the reflections of those who are learning and listening to what those who teach and have already published novels and short

---

1   D.F. Wallace, *Un antidoto contro la solitudine*, Minimum Fax, Rome 2013, p. 25. An excellent all-round portrait is that drawn by P. Arden, *David Foster Wallace carbura*, in the volume just cited, pp. 164-74.

stories have to say? Writing and teaching are thus the two pillars of the most important activity in his life, albeit short and marked by the demon of depression. When one writes one must, according to Wallace, give something to the reader; so that when one reads one ends the reading richer than when one began it. This enrichment that one gives one's readers distinguish artists from tradesmen, those who write for themselves and others from those who write to make money.

The DFW character - as it is often referred to, in the manner of Roosvelt, FDR and Kennedy, JFK - is in some respects comparable to that of Glenn Gould: both are partly constructed by the press, TV, radio, critics and specialist journals, partly self-created.

The Wallace family almost resembles the Glass family as told by Sa- linger: the parents are intelligent and cultured, middle-class people from the Midwest, in America between the rebellious and countercultural 1960s and the 1970s of depression and low national esteem around the defeat in Vietnam, the Watergate scandal and the oil crisis. For the young boy David, childhood flows in an almost muffled universe, with his parents reading Joyce's *Ulysses* hand in hand in bed at night, in an unpretentious flat but loaded with books and literary magazines.

Father, mother, and sister do not immediately realise that the young boy at just ten years of age begins to suffer from 'depressive feelings and pathological anxiety', from a kind of 'impostor syndrome', terrified by the conviction that he does not live up to his parents' excessively high expectations. But the facts soon proved him wrong, with above-average school results and an early inclination for philosophy and literature. At Amherst College he shows himself eclectic and even genial, earning envy, esteem and admiration from classmates and fellow students.

In essence, not only or not so much what the world says about him as what he believes the world says about him is perhaps the main constant of his literary life - at least in his early days. The fact that he has become a highly prized, sometimes deified, prolific author without failing to meet the criteria of profound inspiration and absolute seriousness is due to his extraordinary willpower, introspection (which has its counterpart in hypersensitivity), and the prevalence of self-confidence over phases of unquestionable self-criticism.

Already in his second year of college, he wrote regularly: so it was 27 years dedicated first and foremost to literature and yielded almost 20 volumes, including novels, collections of short stories and essays, articles in the press and interviews. But what he often calls 'the bad thing', depression, he knows will never leave him. Of himself he says that in his 20s he spends his time studying and playing tennis, writing, and reading Wittgenstein and Pynchon, treating himself with Tofranil and 'farting around, swimming a bit' and flirting when he feels confident enough. As for the Austrian-British philosopher, he represents a decisive reference point for the 20-year-old writer and essayist. While he is writing his first novel, *The Broom of the System*, he devotes himself to his bachelor's thesis, choosing philosophy as a subject.

The implications of Wittgenstein's theories were both living and pulsating matter: after all, the late Wittgenstein corresponded to the healthy Wallace; the early Wittgenstein to the author in the grip of depression. The novel and the thesis in Philosophy were two sides of the same coin: both questioned whether language merely described the world or whether it came more decisively to define and shape it.[2]

Thus, language is one of the sources of one's being a writer. It is therefore interesting to mention the editing process of the first novel, the aforementioned *The Broom of the System*, which came out in January 1987.

For his agent, Bonnie Nadell, his editor, Gerry Howard of Viking Penguin, and for many reading the manuscript of the novel, Wallace might finally represent the long-awaited alternative to the minimalism that prevailed in the Eighties of American letters. At first meeting, the unkempt beard and U2 t-shirt, the author's young age (23) and naïve manner surprised the seasoned editorial consultant to no small degree - suffice it to mention that Howard is the editor of *Gravity's Rainbow*, considered to be Thomas Pynchon's masterpiece. After a few months of work, he sends no less than four pages to the young

---

2   D.T. Max, *Ogni storia d'amore è una storia di fantasmi. Vita di David Foster Wallace*, Einaudi, Turin 2013, pp. 72-73.

writer, considering himself to have been rather bland and moderate
- if one takes into account the length of the manuscript (the book in
the Italian edition runs to exactly 500 pages).

But for Wallace in the early days, the slightest criticism puts him
off. Responding to Howard, he rebukes him for having spent the time
eating and smoking intensively because of him, although he is willing
to go back over many passages indicated by the editor. Overall,
Wallace behaves honestly: he contains his neurotic temperament,
backtracks on his own positions in the face of Howard's experience
and foresight and accepts his criticism.

Let's look at some illuminating examples of the relationship
between the two:

> there was a pun on the names of Raymond Carver and Max Apple,
> a comic writer. 'The Carver/Apple jokes are too witty, they will
> come back to haunt you. Cut them,' Howard suggested, and Wallace
> did. Howard believed his author had misused the suspensory dots in
> inverted commas to indicate the absence of a verbal response, a pause
> for silence in the dialogue's exchange of lines. Wallace diminished their
> recurrence. (…)[3]

But when Howard wants the digressions that the character of the
psychotherapist Dr. Jay indulges in to be toned down, Wallace gets
angry. He resents, in other words, being accused of 'literarily beating
around the bush' or of being negligent. In general, all the editors
who work with the author of *Infinite Jest* find him exaggeratedly
deferential and condescending, going so far as to wonder if he is not
pulling their leg. Biographer Max argues that this is true and not true
at the same time.

At the time, for Wallace, Howard represented the man who had
agreed to bet on his first effort, and any gratitude would never repay
that gesture. But Wallace was certainly not lacking in guile. He was
already planning to publish a sequel to the novel, a collection of short
stories, and it was not prudent to reject his editor - or his readers, for
that matter - before he even had any. So, motivated by sincerity - or

---

3   Max, *Ogni storia d'amore…*, cit. p. 109.

some form of sincerity, or perhaps none at all - he wrote to Howard (...) reassured him.[4]

Let us look at another example of literary and human relations with publishing consultants, pages that are fundamental to understanding David Foster Wallace as a writer. After hitting rock bottom in 1990 - as he himself writes to his closest friends - the following year he managed to teach three courses at Emerson College (where he was an adjunct lecturer for a few years); even though he had practically no relationship with his colleagues or students, outside of his teaching duties - which he performed, as always, to the best of his ability. After an emergency hospitalisation, he is forced to depend for many years on Nardil, a neuroleptic that proves to be a kind of life-saver, as it enables him to write, teach, travel and live normally. So much so that he writes to his agent that he feels he is more of a writer than he wanted to be in 1985, while inviting her not to give him up, neither humanly nor artistically.

In 1992, he happily cohabited with his partner, almost thought he was living on writing alone, and managed to teach as usual with excellent results. In terms of literature, he deeply admires Cormac McCarthy and Don DeLillo, has a sort of cult for Carver and has one of the most intense friendships of his life with Franzen. Psychologically, he gets better, takes the saviour Nardil and attends Alcoholics Anonymous, while he starts a psychoanalytic course with good results. As a writer, he is objectively matured, and feels so himself - when the demon of low self-esteem does not visit him.

We have now reached the fourth book (after *The Broom of the System, Girl with Curious Hair* and the one on rap written four-hands with his friend Mark Costello), for many the most mature and rich. The elaboration of *Infinite Jest* is definitely appropriate in terms of time compared to its disproportionate length (the Italian edition amounts to exactly 1278 pages). This time it is Michael Pietsch who is in charge of the editorial work on Wallach's enormous work, starting with the first 750 manuscript sheets in May '93. With remarkable perspicacity he communicates his enthusiasm to the author, with the

---

4   Ibid, p. 111.

only limitation, for now, being the exaggerated length - would a big book of over 1200 pages sell, Pietsch legitimately asks himself?

The second aspect is the so-called 'physics' of the book:

> The fragmentary nature of the book - three narrative lines alternating without a recognisable pattern - was perhaps too much. A certain degree of in- novation was a good thing, but overdoing it risked losing the reader along the way. This was the most difficult aspect to solve for Wallace, who had decided to deliberately confuse the readers' expectations: if contemporary reality was fragmented, the novel had to be too. And the structural choice also corresponded to another conviction of Wallace's: the story should not be entertaining enough to recreate the disease he was trying to diagnose. It did not have to captivate with immediate expedients.[5]

Reading these convictions of Wallace's seems to be a literary interpretation of the reflections contained in the famous chapter on the culture industry in Adorno and Horkheimer's masterpiece. And to find confirmation of the theory on culture in mass society elaborated half a century earlier by the Frankfurt School gives a thrill of pleasure to those who feel far removed from a today marked by inauthenticity and injustice passed off as human destiny:

> The triumph of the beautiful is realised by humour, by the malignant pleasure one feels at the sight of each happily successful deprivation. One laughs at the fact that there is nothing to laugh about.
> Hilarity interrupts and nullifies the pleasure that could theoretically be provided by the spectacle of the embrace, and postpones actual satisfaction until the day of the pogrom.[6]

The ability shown by the young writer to hold on to his project, in the face of the mercantile expectations that the publishing industry might impose on him, is an unequivocal demonstration of the distance between sincere, authentic literature (and art, culture in general) and the pure commodity of the culture factories.

---

5   Ibid, pp. 292-93.
6   M. Horkheimer and T.W. Adorno, *Dialettica dell'illuminismo*, Einaudi, Turin 1966,
pp. 145-48.

4.2 *I am not a grunge writer. Wallace: the novel as a cure*

When the big book appears in bookshops, it amounts to 1080 pages. For a historical period just a few years away from the double end - century and millennium - one would have expected a sort of snapshot of this turning point that intrigues, attracts, frightens (remember the terror of the Y2K hoax, the 'madness' of computers). Wallace, on the other hand, goes its own way, arousing esteem, admiration, and perplexity. Obscure, too long, difficult to understand: however, most of the criticism is positive.

The harshest review is by the renowned (and much-feared) Japanese- born New York Times veteran, Michiko Kakutani. The critic of the most prestigious US newspaper makes a Wallace incapable of arrogance and self-assurance suffer greatly - although a dose of venom is aimed at the editor. Kakutani immediately expresses her doubt that she has read the masterpiece that many claim she is:

> The book seems to have been written and edited (or perhaps not edited) on the general principle that bigger is better, that more means more important, and the result is therefore a psychedelic jumble of characters, anecdotes, stories, soliloquies, reminiscences, and echoes that is as bombastic and astonishing as it is arbitrary and complacent.[7]

It should also be remembered that part of the author's success while still alive, especially in the mid-1990s, is due to the misunderstanding of mistaking him for the literary spokesman of the grunge generation, linked to the Seattle music movement (two names for all: Nirvana and Pearl Jam). But Max's biographical sketch captures at least a couple of aspects that are indeed common: an aggressive and uncomfortable sincerity in the face of the contemporary world, together with an allergy to hypocrisy and creepiness, the cult of the facade, of form without substance - from politics to advertising, from business to culture. Wallace is annoyed at being lumped together to the young ne'er-do-wells and reefers, with their jeans ripped off at the knees and their lumberjack flannel shirts in colourful checks - so much so that he denied ever having

---

7   Ibid, p. 346.

heard of Nirvana (hard to believe him, he so intrigued by everything in the art world, including pop music).

Yet Max seems to be right when he observes:

> As Wallace stated in an interview at the time: 'In a way, it seems to me that reality at the moment is smashed to smithereens. At least the reality that I live in'. The refrain of Smells Like Teen Spirit and Wallace's portrait of a media- addicted generation ran along the same lines: 'I feel stupid and contagious [...] Here we are now, entertain us'.[8]

But what does DFW think of fellow writers? He devotes numerous pages to American (and a few European) storytellers. One essay in particular is devoted to the question of minimalism: a question in the sense of fame, exhibition, easy assimilation (we have seen this for Carver), enthusiastic criticism (actually with some disagreements) and above all being absolutely fashionable in the midst of the 1980s. Reagan is in power and ideology as a concept is put in the attic, the buzzword is "get rich!" while the most accredited social figure is the yuppie (young urban professional), the single person is for the first time courted by the consumer industry and many couples of *yuppies* theorise about not having children in order to devote themselves entirely to career, money and social success. Minimalism serves as a powerful literary backdrop to this social landscape full of shadows - the first one to emerge in 1982/83 is AIDS, which wipes out the legacy of the sexual revolution of the previous two decades. With ill-concealed irony Wallace speaks of 'conspicuously young' writers in crisis with respect to the literary Establishment - he is writing at the end of the decade, in 1988.

Here is how he summarises and classifies what he calls 'sleazy strands':

> (1) Nihilism (...) trumpeted through Yuppies with six-figure salaries and their offspring with artificial tans and non-existent morality (...)

---

8   Ibid, pp. 352-53. Of Nirvana's splendid hit *Smells Like Teen Spirit*, an authentic generational manifesto, compare the electric and acoustic versions respectively on the records: 1991's *Nevermind* and 1994's *Unplugged in New York* (the latter is a live performance that appeared a few months before the death of the charismatic leader Kurt Cobain).

(2) Catatonic Realism also known as Ultraminimalism also known as Carver's Misguided, where suburbs are dumps, adults automatons and narrators opaque perceptual engines (...)

(3) Workshop Hermeticism (...) narrative on which the pre- and proscriptions of the Writing Programme loom with the occlusive force of horizons[9]

The young writer's attack on the allegedly *nerdy* (as they used to say in those years about the sloppily dressed, unsportsmanlike, long-haired, bespectacled upperclassmen) is directed against inauthenticity, being fashionable, the use of big words without knowing their meaning (it is no coincidence that he often uses capital letters in the e- list), the uncritical mania of *Creative Writing* courses - claiming to be able to become a Flaubert or Hemingway with a simple bachelor's or master's degree - the pseudo social figures that one absolutely has to tell, neglecting authentic human beings.

Every cultural instrument always has two sides: courses for writers can be an opportunity for growth and self-criticism or a chase after fashions without understanding them; TV is a box for mass dumbing down, but it can be used to learn and deepen, alongside books and other educational material (the same criticism has been valid for more than 20 years with regard to computers); cultural currents of philosophical, literary, linguistic and historical thought must be studied in their complexity, without making them into impeccable gospels.

the wave of Post-Structuralism, Marxism, Feminism, Freudism, Deconstruction, Semiotics, Hermeneutics, and related -isms crosses the American accademy (...) penetrates the consciousness of the conscious adult American.[10]

According to Wallace, DeLillo conceives of the novel as a child to be raised and cared for with care (in *Mao II*), while Pynchon is capable of showing where transcendence can lead (in the case of *Gravity's Rainbow*), in this similar to the poet Milton; *Towards the End of Time* analyses Updike's novel with greater lucidity than Roth's acrimony towards the author of the Rabbitt cycle, and it is

---

9   D.F. Wallace, *Di carne e di nulla*, Einaudi, Turin 2012, p. 92.
10   Ibid, p. 116.

an essay immediately followed by pages that illuminate humour in Kafka like few others. It is curious to note how the Prague writer is admired and sometimes idolised by many contemporary American novelists - one thinks of Roth who devoted some splendid lectures to him in the 1970s.[11]

As for Dostoevsky, he dedicates an entire essay to him based on the studies of Joseph Frank, a Slavist lecturer at Princeton. And also in this twenty pages one is almost astonished by the contrast in Wallace between the depressed novelist, alcoholic for years, extravagant in his dress and treatment of his subjects (outbursts of affection and periods of catatonic isolation) and the sharp, erudite essayist, precise to the point of mania in his footnotes, yet capable of irony and shrewd humour. A small example when he writes that

> By now, Professor Frank must be about seventy-five years old, and judging by the photo on the back cover of The Miraculous Years, he is not exactly sprightly.
> 3. The amount of hours he must have spent in the library would take the vigour out of anyone, I imagine[12]

What remains of such a character is the sadness of not being able to hear or read about him anymore. In 2007, he suddenly decided to stop taking Nardil, which had lasted about twenty years. The absence of the neuroleptic caused increasing crises, even though Wallace was as successful as ever in conducting his brilliant university courses and seminars. Unfortunately, no other antidepressant can be found without Nardil's contraindications (primarily the induction of high hypertension).

The last year of David's life alternates between nervous breakdowns, severe stomach pains, bewilderment, and the administration of no fewer than 12 electro-shock sessions (so much for experiences such as the anti- psychiatry of Laing and Cooper or the radical critical psychiatry movement of Basaglia and his school). The outcome feared and postponed for years finally occurs.

---

11   See P. Roth, *"Ho sempre volute che ammiraste il mio digiuno", Ovvero, guardando Kafka*, Einaudi, Turin 2011.
12   D.F. Wallace, *Considera l'aragosta*, Einaudi, Turin 2005, p. 286.

One day Karen left David home alone with the dogs for a few hours. Upon entering that evening, she found him hanging.

"I can't get this image out of my head," says the sister. "David and the dogs, in the dark. I'm sure he kissed them on the mouth, and apologised."[13]

That concluding 'image' is a little gem of perfidy.

---

13   D.F. Wallace, *Un antidoto contro la solitudine*, Minimum Fax, Rome 2013, p. 292.

TERRIBLE, DEAR FAMILY.
FRANZEN SOCIAL PATHOLOGIST

The family microcosm identifies with the entire American society and the inevitable fallacy of 'corrections' highlights the drama of a trapped society.[1]

Write sentences so authentic that one can find refuge in them.[2]

One can trace the poetics of a novelist and essayist like Jonathan Franzen thanks to these two considerations dating back to the years of his first (great) literary success, thanks to the novel *The Corrections*. A work that is already his third, published for one of those pure cases that feed the history of literature (and culture in general) just a few days after the attacks on the Twin Towers in New York and the Pentagon in Washington. And that an entire country, a federation made up of 50 states and more than 270 million people (in 2001), with a very high rate of immigrants from five continents, born only in 1776, manages to recover from a tragedy like that of September 11 even appreciating a novel like *The Corrections* seems to us a measure of great beauty to understand the rich complexity of that country.

It is also true that Franzen is anything but clueless and conformist, with the public representing an entirely generic entity, the reader is a social isolate, publishing reasons and operates largely as a kind of Hollywood subsidiary, not art but success dominates unchallenged in the United States.[3]

---

1   A. Monda, *America. Sguardi tristi*, La Repubblica newspaper, 4 January 2002.

2   J. Franzen, *Come stare soli. Lo scrittore, il lettore e la cultura di massa*, Einaudi, Turin 2003, p. 84.

3   See the respective quotations on pp. 75, 174, 77, 85, 92, in Franzen, *Come stare soli...*, cit.

But after two novels (*The Twenty-Seventh City* and *Strong Motion*) that were not very well received by the public and critics, he even tried the route of the great American novel - a book form with which characters from the likes of Roth with *American Pastoral*, John Updike and the four episodes of the *Rabbit-Rabbitt* cycle, Don De Lillo writing *Underworld*.

Franzen may have had the ambition to write the Great American Novel, but where did it come from? That is, what does his book look like? Let me quote a sentence: 'What I ran into was an old boot full of pride stuck at the bottom of a stagnant lake of academic boredom, the typical, instinctive self- censoring attitude of any real enthusiasm'. Well: this sentence is not by Franzen, but by Jonathan Lethem, a writer of his age. But Franzen could have written it. And so they are, each with their own peculiarities. Michael Cunningham, David Foster Wallace and George Saunders, Michael Chabon and Dave Eggers: stylistically brilliant, inclined to metaphorize, to make psychology plastic, or concrete. This is the constant of American literature in the 1990s: which has none of the typical characteristics of postmodernism and which in fact stems from the minimalist experience of the 1980s, from Bret Easton Ellis to Donna Tartt. (...) the American novel has emerged from its classicism.[4]

In wanting to write a memorable novel, one that marks a milestone (as they say in English), there is a combination of ambition, frustration, a challenge to oneself and to other writers, the conviction of possessing that talent mentioned at the beginning of the book, and the obstinacy to overcome the crisis in the dialogue with culture - which Franzen himself speaks of in a fine essay following *The Corrections*.[5] But the writer must not place himself in a snobbish elitism, while he must perceive himself as different and better than the works intended f o r today's market pseudo literary.

---

4   F. Cordelli, *La famiglia tradita dal sogno americano*, Corriere della sera quotidiano, 24 April 2002.

5   "The novelist has more and more things to say to readers who have less and less time to read them. Where to find the energy to dialogue with a culture in crisis when the crisis consists in the impossibility of dialogue with culture?" Franzen, *Come stare soli*, cit., p. 65.

In the illuminating essay *Why Write Novels?* from 1996 Franzen argues against to the idea of literature as a noble higher calling, because elitism doesn't sit well with my American nature, and because (...) my faith in good manners would make it difficult for me to explain to my brother, who is a Michael Crichton fan, that my work is simply better than Crichton's. (...) I know there was a reason why I liked reading and I liked writing. But every apologia and every defence seem to dissolve in the churning water of contemporary culture, and soon it will become really difficult to get out of bed in the morning.[6]

The author of *The Corrections* has for several years been polemical about the mass techno-culture that fills the Western (and non-Western) world and contributes to its globalisation - with both positive and negative results. This well-defined and sincere orientation of the writer from St. Louis is not without controversy. Such as when he refuses to be a guest on the TV lounge of the very powerful Oprah Winfrey - only to later change his mind. What emerges in these *querelles* is a man who is at times contradictory, certainly hypersensitive (he would probably not be a writer in the first place), with human traits that link him to his great friend David Foster Wallace.[7]

There is a profound conviction that despite all the devilry (good and bad) with which the electronic and computer revolution of recent decades has filled shops and homes, writing, reading, and imagining remain and will remain in any case. As Franzen writes intensely: when the world is ending and continues to end, it is good to know that you still belong to it.

After all, one of the gurus of the computer revolution, Nicholas Negroponte, a professor at MIT in Boston, speaks of the book as

---

6   Ibid, p. 74.
7   "Today for every reader who dies there is a spectator who is born (...) the transition from a culture based on virtual images - a transition that began with television and is being completed with the computer - is an apocalyptic fact". Franzen, *Come stare soli*, cit., p. 165. Two valuable accounts of Wallace's friendship and esteem for Franzen and vice versa can be found in: Max, *Ogni storia d'amore*, cit., pp. 183, 265-67, 418; J. Franzen, *L'isola più lontana*, in *Più lontano ancora*, Einaudi, Turin 2012, pp. 15-48. The essay first appeared in Italian in the weekly L'Internazionale, August/September 2006.

a stimulator of the imagination, unlike interactive multimedia that leaves very little room for imagination.

While novels are by no means defunct, it is unquestionable that the role that the novel form has played for centuries is increasingly disappearing. The novel as the seat of cultural authority, writes Franzen, the book as the catalyst of fulfilment for the reader (and even more so for the writer) is faltering, while the 'author's domain', that social function that the writer has performed throughout the entire modern era and which constitutes the purpose of reading and writing, is waning.[8]

But beyond the cultural and social aspect, there is the individual aspect whereby reading is one of those acts that guarantees being alone, being able to deal with one's loneliness and at the same time a way out. It is not for nothing that the title of this collection of essays is *How to be Alone*.

As he says in an interview:

> I have my doubts about the fact that a fiction writer has to hunt for material. (...) quality fiction is born out of confrontation with oneself. (...) the world invests us anyway, whether we want it to or not. Maybe because a friend dies. Or because he falls ill (...) That's when I find myself with a story to write (...) I don't care if I have to be alone for the rest. I have to be alone to separate the useful signals from the noise. I have to listen to fewer things, to hear better.[9]

---

8   "There is a general tendency to confuse techniques with their applications in a given society (...) much of what we call communication is in itself, necessarily, nothing more than transmission: that is, a sending in one direction. If our purpose is art, education, the transmission of information or opinion, our interpretation will be in the terms of being rational and interested. If, on the other hand, our purpose is to influence - to persuade a large number of people to act, feel, think, and know in a certain way - the appropriate formula will be that of the masses'. R. Williams, *Cultura e rivoluzione industriale. Inghilterra 1780-1950*, Einaudi, Turin 1968, pp. 349, 356-57, 358-59.

9   J. Franzen, *Solo, dunque scrivo. Intervista* di Livia Manera, Corriere della sera daily newspaper, 22 May 2004. On this theme, see also J. Franzen, *Perché ho scelto di stare da solo. Intervista* di Antonio Monda, La Repubblica, 22 December 2002.

BIBLIOGRAPHICAL REFERENCES

AA.VV., *Dizionario universale della letteratura contemporanea*. 5 volumes, Mondadori, Milan 1959.

Lucilla Albano, *La caverna dei giganti. Scritti sull'evoluzione del dispositivo cinematografico*, Pratiche Editrice, Turin 1992.

Martin Amis, *Il mio Roth. L'uomo che fa di se stesso un romanzo*, La Repubblica daily, 20 November 2013.

Angelo Aquaro, *Roth attacca il Nobel: 'Sono dei provinciali'*, La Repubblica quotidian, 19 January 2013.

Paul Auster, *Le trame della scrittura*. Intervista di Matteo Bellinelli, Casagrande, Lugano 2005.

Francesca Baiardi (ed.), *Adesso possiamo cominciare. Philip Roth, una storia americana*, Feltrinelli, Milan 2013.

Piero Bairati (ed.), *Il mondo contemporaneo. Storia del Nord America*, La Nuova Italia, Florence 1978.

Marco Belpoliti, *Quell'apocalissi warholiana di Don De Lillo* (19.07.2003), in *Diario dell'occhio*, Le Lettere, Florence 2008.

Alfonso Berardinelli, *L'incontro con la realtà*, in Franco Moretti (ed.), *Il romanzo. Volume secondo: Le forme*, Einaudi, Turin 2002.

Harold Bloom, *Il canone occidentale. I Libri e le Scuole delle Età*, Bompiani, Milan 1996.

Francesca Borrelli, *Provaci ancora Roth*, Alias Sunday-supplement to Il Manifesto daily, 18 November 2012.

Luca Briasco and Mattia Carratello (eds.), *La letteratura americana dal 1900 a oggi. Dizionario per autori*, Einaudi, Turin 2011.

Maria Rosa Bricchi, *Philip Roth. Biografia nonostante l'autore*, Il Sole 24 ore, 15 December 2013.

Burgess Anthony, *Hemingway*, Editrice Nuova, Milan 1983.

Maddalena Raimondi Capasso and Renata Fiotta Genova, *Cross-Sections. A Socio- Literary Survey of British and American Cultural Traditions*, Ghisetti e Corvi Editori, Milan 1981.

Charles Bukowski, *Donne*, Guanda, Parma 1999.

Raymond Carver, *Il mestiere di scrivere*, Einaudi, Turin 1997.

Raymond Carver, *Intervista*, Minimum Fax, Rome 1996.

Raymond Carver, *Principianti*, Einaudi, Turin 2009.

Raymond Carver, *Di cosa parliamo quando parliamo d'amore*, Garzanti, Milan 1987.

F. Castelli, *Redenzione e perdizione nell'opera di Flannery O'Connor*, in La Civiltà Cattolica, 1994, I, p. 437.

J.M. Coetzee, *On the Moral Brink. Philip Roth, Nemesis*, The New York Review of Books, October 28, 2010.

H.S. Commager, *Lo spirito americano*, La Nuova Italia, Florence 1951.

Stephen Cooper, *Una vita piena. Biografia di John Fante*, Marcos y Marcos, Milano 2011, pp. 36-38.

Franco Cordelli, *La famiglia tradita dal sogno americano*, Corriere della sera quotidiano, 24 April 2002.

Mario Corona, *Cronologia*, in J. Kerouac, *Romanzi e racconti*, Mondadori, Milan 2001.

Ruggero D'Alessandro, *La pensatrice e lo specialista. Hannah Arendt e il processo Eichmann*, Ombre Corte, Verona 2015.

Ruggero D'Alessandro, *La società vistosa. Attualità di Veblen*, Marxist Criticism, bimonthly, September-October 2011, pp. 41-50 (double column).

Maurizio De Benedictis, *Il cinema americano. Dalle origini ai giorni nostri*, Newton Compton Editori, Rome 2005.

Luciano De Fiore, *Roth. Fantasmi del desiderio*, Editori Riuniti, Rome 2012.

Luca Doninelli, *Nessuno prestava attenzione al cielo*, in F. O'Connor, *La saggezza nel sangue*, Garzanti, Milan 2010.

Antonio Donno, *Dal New Deal alla guerra fredda. Aspetti del radicalismo statunitense negli anni '40*, Sansoni Editore, Florence 1983.

Francesco Durante, *Uno dei 'big boys'*, introductory essay to J. Fante, *Romanzi e racconti*, Mondadori, Milan 2003.

Maria Serena Falagiani, *Flannery O'Connor. 'Un cuore al posto giusto*, in F. O'Connor, *La schiena di Parker*, BUR - Rizzoli, Milan 2008.

John Fante, *Lettere 1942-1981*, edited by S. Cooney, Einaudi, Turin 2004.

John Fante, *Romanzi e racconti*, Mondadori, Milan 2003.

William Faulkner, *Pensando a casa. Lettere alla madre e al padre*, edited by J.G. Watson, Rosellina Archinto, Milan 1993.

William Faulkner, *W.F. Scritti, discorsi e lettere*, edited by J.B. Meriwether, Il Saggiatore, Milan 2010.

William Faulkner, *Opere scelte*, edited by F. Pivano, Mondadori, Milan 1995-2004.

Filippetti Antonio, *Jack Kerouac*, Il Castoro, Florence 1975.

Guido Fink, Mario Maffi, Franco Minganti, Bianca Tarozzi, *Storia della letteratura americana*, Sansoni, Florence 2001.

Francis Scott Fitzgerald, *Crepuscolo di uno scrittore*, Mondadori, Milan 1992.

Francis Scott Fitzgerald, *Il grande Gatsby*, Newton Compton Editori, Rome 1989.

Francis Scott Fitzgerald, *Racconti dell'età del jazz*, Mondaddori, Milan 1980.

Francis Scott Fitzgerald, *I taccuini*, Einaudi, Turin 1980.

Jonathan Franzen, *Come stare soli. Lo scrittore, il lettore e la cultura di massa*, Einaudi, Turin 2003.

Jonathan Franzen, *Zona disagio*, Einaudi, Turin 2006.

Jonathan Franzen, *Più lontano ancora*, Einaudi, Turin 2012.

Jonathan Franzen, *L'isola più lontana*, in The Weekly International, August/ September 2006.

Jonathan Franzen, *Solo, dunque scrivo*. Intervista di Livia Manera, Corriere della sera newspaper, 22 May 2004.

Jonathan Franzen, *Perché ho scelto di starmene da solo*. Intervista di Antonio Monda, La Repubblica newspaper, 22 December 2002.

Jonathan Franzen, Intervista di Donald Antrim, Bomb magazine no., 77, fall 2001 (translation by Andrea Bajani and Lorenza Pieri).

Jonathan Franzen, *L'America di J. Franzen*. Intervista di Susanna Battisti, http:// www.kwlibri.kataweb.it/incontro/incontro_230402.shtml.

French Warren, *Steinbeck*, la Nuova Italia, Florence 1969.

Northrop Frye, *Anatomia della critica. Quattro saggi*, Einaudi, Turin 1969.

Franco Garnero, *Invito alla lettura di John Steinbeck*, Mursia, Milan 1999.

Michal Peled Ginsburg and Lorri G. Nandrea, *La prosa del mondo. 4. America terra della prosa: L'americano, Il grande Gatsby*, in Franco Moretti (ed.), *Il romanzo. Volume quarto: Temi, luoghi, eroi*, Einaudi, Turin 2003.

Romano Giachetti, *Il giovane Salinger*, Baldini & Castaldi, Milan 1998.

Sergio Givone, *Dire le emozioni. La costruzione dell'interiorità nel romanzo moderno*, in Franco Moretti (ed.), *Il romanzo. Volume primo: La cultura del romanzo*, Einaudi, Turin 2001.

Claudio Gorlier, *Introduzione*, in Philip Roth, *Il lamento di Portnoy*, Bompiani, Milan 1970.

Frederick J. Hoffman, *Faulkner*, Il Castoro, Florence 1967.

Bruno Monsaingeon, *Glenn Gould. No, non sono un eccentrico*, EDT/Musica, Turin 1989.

Salvatore Guglielmino, *Guida al Novecento*, Principato editore, Milan 1970.

Ian Hamilton, *In cerca di Salinger*, Minimum Fax, Rome 2001.

Ernest Hemingway, *Morte nel pomeriggio*, Mondadori, Milan 1961.

Ernest Hemingway, *Romanzi*, edited by F. Pivano, Mondadori, Milan 1992.

Ernest Hemingway - Agnes Von Kurowski, *In amore e in guerra*, Mursia, Milan 1992, p. 188.

Raul Hilberg, *La distruzione degli Ebrei d'Europa*, 2 volumes, Einaudi, Turin 1995.

Alfred Hitchcock, *Hitchcock secondo Hitchcock. Idee e Confessioni del maestro del brivido*, Baldini &Castaldi, Milan 2000.

Max Horkheimer and Theodor W. Adorno, *Dialettica dell'illuminismo*, Einaudi, Turin 1966.

Johan Huizinga, *Homo ludens. Il gioco come funzione sociale*, Il Saggiatore, Milan 1967.

Maldwyn A. Jones, *Storia degli Stati Uniti. Dalle prime colonie inglesi ai giorni nostri*, Bompiani, Milan 1995.

Jack Kerouac, *Intervista*, Minimum Fax, Rome 1998.

Jack Kerouac, *Romanzi e racconti*, Mondadori, Milan 2001.

Jack Kerouac, *Un mondo battuto dal vento. I diari 1947/1954*, Mondadori, Milan 2006.

Edie Kerouac-Parker, *La mia vita con Jack*, Stampa alternativa, Rome 2008.

Livia Manera, *Jonathan Franzen: solo dunque scrivo*, D insert of the Corriere della sera daily, 22 May 2004.

Eric Lomazoff, *The Praises and Criticisms of J.D. Salinger's The Catcher in Rye*, 1996, http://www.levity.com/corduroy/salinger1.htm.

Vittorio Macioce, *C'era una volta la famiglia americana*, Il Giornale quotidiano, 17 April 2001.

Simona Magherini, *Introduzione* in Jerome Salinger, Hapworth 16, 1924, Eldonejo, Milan 1997.

F.O. Matthiessen, *Le responsabilità del critico*, Feltrinelli, Milan 1966.

D.T. Max, *Ogni storia d'amore è una storia di fantasmi. Vita di David Foster Wallace*, Einaudi, Turin 2013.

Paolo Mereghetti, *Dizionario dei film 2011. vol. A-L*, Baldini Castaldi Dalai, Milan 2010.

Paolo Mereghetti, *Dizionario dei film 2011. vol. M-Z*, Baldini Castaldi Dalai, Milan 2010.

Antonio Monda, *America. Sguardi tristi*, La Repubblica newspaper, 4 January 2002.

Antonio Monda, *Buon compleanno, Mr. Roth*, La Repubblica newspaper, 13 March 2013.

Franco Moretti, *Opere mondo. Saggio sulla forma epica dal Faust a Cent anni di solitudine*, Einaudi, Turin 1994.

Franco Moretti, *La letteratura vista da lontano*, Einaudi, Turin 2005.

Gigliola Nocera, *L'America profonda di Raymond Carvver's* and *Cronologia* in Raymond Carver, *Racconti*, Mondadori, Milan 2005.

Flannery O'Connor, *Sola a presidiare la Fortezza. Lettere*, edited by O. Fatica, Einaudi, Turin 2001.

Flannery O'Connor, *Nel territorio del diavolo*, Minimum fax, Rome 2003.

Flannery O'Connor, *La saggezza nel sangue*, Garzanti, Milan 2010.

Flannery O'Connor, *Il cielo è dei violenti*, Einaudi, Turin 2008.

Flannery O'Connor, *Tutti i racconti*, Bompiani, Milan 2009.

Flannery O'Connor, *Il volto incompiuto. Saggi e lettere sul mestiere di scrivere*, edited by A. Spadaro, BUR - Rizzoli, Milan 2011.

Osimo Bruno, *There's no there there*, in J. Steinbeck, *L'America e gli americani e altri scritti*, edited by B. Osimo, Alet Edizioni, Padua 2008, pp. 9- 13.

Cesare Pavese, *La letteratura americana e altri saggi*, Einaudi, Turin 1951.

Alessandro Piperno, *Lettera aperta a Enzo Siciliano sul caso Philip Roth*, in Nuovi Argomenti Quarterly, July/September 2003, pp. 93/121.

Fernanda Pivano, *Prefazione* a *Gli ultimi fuochi di Francis Scott Fitzgerald*, Mondadori, Milan 1952.

Fernanda Pivano, *L'"età del jazz". Prefazione* a *Belli e dannati* di Francis Scott Fitzgerald, Mondadori, Milan 1954.

Fernanda Pivano, *Amici scrittori. Quarant'anni di incontri e scoperte con gli autori americani*, Mondadori, Milan 1995.

Fernanda Pivano, *Beat Hippie Yippie. Il romanzo del pre-sessantotto americano*, Bompiani, Milan 1990.

Fernanda Pivano, *Cronologia*, in E. Hemingway, *Romanzi*, edited by F. Pivano,

Mondadori, Milan 1992.

Fernanda Pivano, *La balena bianca e altri miti*, Il Saggiatore, Milan 1995.

Fernanda Pivano, *Album americano*, Frassinelli, Milan 1997.

Fernanda Pivano, *Viaggio americano*, Bompiani, Milan 2001.

Fernanda Pivano, *Cronologia*, in W. Faulkner, *Opere scelte*, edited by F. Pivano, Mondadori, Milan 1995-2004.

Fernanda Pivano, *Pagine americane*, Frassinelli, Milan 2005.

Alessandro Portelli, *Nel segno della voce. Oralità e scrittura negli Stati Uniti*, in Franco Moretti (ed.), *Il romanzo. Volume terzo: Storia e geografia*, Einaudi, Turin 2002.

David Remnick, *Philip Roth Says Enough*, The New Yorker, November 9, 2012.

Gianni Rondolino, *Storia del cinema*, UTET, Turin 1995.

Philip Roth, *I fatti. Autobiografia di un romanziere*, Leonardo, Milan 1989.

Philip Roth, *Guardando Kafka*, Einaudi, Turin 2011.

Philip Roth, *Chiacchiere di bottega. Uno scrittore, i suoi colleghi e il loro lavoro*, Einaudi, Turin 2004.

Philip Roth, *Difensore della fede*, in *Goodbye, Columbus*, Einaudi, Turin 2012, pp. 135-168.

Philip Roth, *"Che bella la vita quando non devi più passarla a scrivere"*. *Intervista* di Cynthia Haven, The Daily Republic, 22 February 2014.

Philip Roth, *"Perché è finita la mia lotta con la scrittura"*. *Intervista* di Carles McGrath, La Repubblica newspaper, 19 November 2012.

Philip Roth, *Al mio maestro*, La Repubblica daily, 5 May 2013.

Claudia Pierpont Roth, *Roth Unbound. A man and his books*, Jonathan Cape, 2013.

Eileen Romano (ed.), *Album Hemingway*, Mondadori, Milan 1988.

Edward Said, *Sullo stile tardo*, Il Saggiatore, Milan 2009.

Jerome Salinger, *The Catcher in the Rye*, Penguin Books, London & New York 1951.

Jerome Salinger, *Il giovane Holden*, Einaudi, Turin 1961.

Jerome Salinger, *Nove racconti*, Einaudi, Turin 1962.

Cinzia Scarpino, Cinzia Schiavini, Sostene M. Zangari, *Guida alla letteratura degli Stati Uniti. Percorsi e protagonisti 1945-2014*, Odoya, Bologna 2014.

Cesare Segre, *Introduzione all'edizione italiana*, in Wolfgang Iser, *L'atto della lettura. Una teoria della risposta estetica*, Il Mulino, Bologna 1987.

David Shields and Shane Salerno, *Salinger. La guerra privata di uno scrittore*, Isbn editions, Milan 2014.

Spadaro Antonio, *La letteratura nel territorio del diavolo. La poetica di Flannery O'Connor*, in La Civiltà Cattolica, 2001, IV, pp. 36-45.

Spadaro Antonio, *"Non sono scrittrice dell'impercettibile, io". Il mistero di Flannery O'Connor*, in O'Connor Flannery, *Il volto incompiuto. Saggi e lettere sul mestiere di scrivere*, edited by A. Spadaro, BUR - Rizzoli, Milan 2011.

John Steinbeck, *La luna è tramontata*, Mondadori, Milan 2004.

John Steinbeck, *L'America e gli americani e altri scritti*, edited by B. Osimo,

Alet Edizioni, Padua 2008, pp. 9-13.

John Steinbeck, *I nomadi*, Il Saggiatore, Milan 2015.

George Steiner, *Vere presenze*, Garzanti, Milan 1998.

Mario Vargas Llosa, *È possibile pensare il mondo moderno senza il romanzo?*, in Franco Moretti (a cura di), *Il romanzo. Volume primo: La cultura del romanzo*, Einaudi, Turin 2001.

Thorstein Veblen, *La teoria della classe agiata*, Einaudi, Turin 1971.

David Foster Wallace, *Di carne e di nulla*, Einaudi, Turin 2012.

David Foster Wallace, *Un antidoto contro la solitudine*, Minimum Fax, Rome 2013.

David Foster Wallace, *Considera l'aragosta*, Einaudi, Turin 2005.

Raymond Williams, *Cultura e rivoluzione industriale. Inghilterra 1780-1950*, Einaudi, Turin 1968.

Edmund Wilson, *Il cronista letterario. Scritti scelti dai "Saggi letterari" e da "Il pensiero multiplo"*. Edited by Grazia Cherchi, Garzanti, Milan 1992.

Giovanna Zucconi, *Incubi americani prima delle torri*, La Stampa newspaper, 23 October 2001.

Giovanna Zucconi, *Lo strambo dell'America*, La Stampa newspaper, 17 April 2002.

MIMESIS GROUP
www.mimesis-group.com

MIMESIS INTERNATIONAL
www.mimesisinternational.com
info@mimesisinternational.com

MIMESIS EDIZIONI
www.mimesisedizioni.it
mimesis@mimesisedizioni.it

ÉDITIONS MIMÉSIS
www.editionsmimesis.fr
info@editionsmimesis.fr

MIMESIS COMMUNICATION
www.mim-c.net

MIMESIS EU
www.mim-eu.com

Printed by
Rotomail Italia S.p.A.
May 2024